THE
GLOBAL
SPEAKER

THE GLOBAL SPEAKER

An English Speaker's Guide to Making Presentations Around the World

Patricia L. Kurtz

American Management Association

New York • Atlanta • Boston • Chicago • Kansas City • San Francisco • Washington, D.C.
Brussels • Mexico City • Tokyo • Toronto

This book is available at a special
discount when ordered in bulk quantities.
For information, contact Special Sales Department,
AMACOM, a division of American Management Association,
135 West 50th Street, New York, NY 10020.

This publication is designed to provide accurate and authoritative
information in regard to the subject matter covered. It is sold with the
understanding that the publisher is not engaged in rendering legal,
accounting, or other professional service. If legal advice or other
expert assistance is required, the services of a competent professional
person should be sought.

Library of Congress Cataloging-in-Publication Data

Kurtz, Patricia L.
    The global speaker : an English speaker's guide to making
presentations around the world / Patricia L. Kurtz.
        p. cm.
    Includes index.
    ISBN 0-8144-7878-6
    1. Public speaking. I. Title.
PN4121.K97   1995
808.5'1—dc20   94-41560
                                                     CIP

Printing number

10   9   8   7   6   5   4   3   2   1

Contents

Acknowledgments

Alerting English speakers to the need to take more responsibility to make ourselves understood when we communicate internationally with people who are not mother-tongue-English is an undertaking that was encouraged by my European clients. I am grateful to all of them for their assistance in this project, but most of all, I want to thank Mr. Franco Reali and his employees at Bertelsmann Music Group, Italy, who have been my teachers as well as my students.

I assume responsibility for all of the recommendations in this book, while simultaneously acknowledging the tremendous debt I owe to my former colleagues at Decker Communications, Inc., where I learned, practiced, and taught "what works" in communications. I especially thank Bert Decker for his permission to adapt The Decker Grid System™ as an example of how to organize a presentation.

Two additional bouquets: first to Maria Jutasi Coleman, who encouraged and supported me to write this book instead of just talk about it, and second to Sandy Boucher, who urged me to take that final step of sending it to a publisher.

THE GLOBAL SPEAKER

1

Introduction

Does the world really need another book on public speaking? Is there anything new to say that hasn't already been adequately said? Have we discovered any great new techniques to communicate more effectively or are we just talking about gimmicky versions of techniques as old as Aristotle? Is there a revolutionary theory about how audiences process information or can we only recycle and paraphrase what we already know?

Until several years ago, I would have suggested a ban on any new books on public speaking as an admirable target for ecology experts bent on saving trees. I had worked for a decade as director of training and product development for one of the foremost communication skill-training companies in the United States. In addition to conducting seminars and individual consultations on how to be a more effective public speaker, I was also responsible for reviewing newly published books. Topics ranged from how to come across like Mother Teresa during a press conference concerning your company's recent environmental disaster, to how to make sure an errant strand of dental floss isn't dangling from your suit lapel throughout the course of your presentation.

I recognized that if you were to multiply the millions of business and professional presentations given every year by the quotient of nervousness and incompetence that accompany them, the market for public speaking books might well be inexhaustible. Nevertheless, I wasn't persuaded that there was anything new to say, and I certainly wouldn't have considered writing a book myself. But then I began to work as a language and communications consultant in Europe and soon discovered a need so large, yet so camouflaged, that I had to encounter it repeatedly before I could accurately identify it.

My European clients are all top-level corporate executives and professionals who speak English as a foreign language. After six months of listening to them berate their ability to understand mother-tongue English speakers, I decided to attend several meetings as an observer. I soon realized that the problem was less my clients' inability to understand native English speakers and more the inability of native English speakers to make themselves understood. Since my clients had less difficulty understanding other foreign speakers of English, I became convinced that the major responsibility for many misfired communications lay with native English speakers. I also noticed that my clients had little difficulty understanding me, so I asked myself what I, as a native speaker of English, had in common with non-native speakers of English. The answer was that I had had to labor to understand and to be understood in a foreign language above and beyond the tourist level of "Where's the bathroom?" and "I'd like ketchup with my fries."

Most native English speakers, however, have never had to function extensively in a foreign language, whereas the number of people who are obligated to learn to communicate in English is ever-increasing. With the collapse of the Berlin Wall, the liberation of Eastern Europe, the end of the Cold War, the economic and political unification of Western Europe, and the signing of NAFTA (North American Free Trade Agreement), the term *global village* has graduated from a hackneyed phrase to a complex reality. In addition, the delicate balance of the international economy, the fragile state of the planetary environment, and problems of worldwide dimensions, such as the proliferation of illicit drugs, organized crime, and the AIDS epidemic, are only a sample of the historic and social realities that have made explicit the interdependence of peoples. The bumper sticker of the 1980s, *Think globally and act locally,* has given way to a need in the 1990s to *Think globally and act globally.*

Though the global thinking that is taking place occurs in many languages, the results of this thinking must often be communicated in English, the international language. In fact, approximately one billion people, equal to one-quarter of the global population, do speak English as a foreign or a second language. It is the language of business and diplomacy. It is the language pilots speak to air controllers at airports throughout the world. It is the foreign language most studied in schools, universities, and language institutes in every latitude and longitude of our planet. The good news is that as English-speaking tourists, we can get lost in virtually any corner of the world and have our anxieties allayed (or exacerbated) by someone who speaks "a little English." The bad news is that because of this cushioned experience, native English speakers have placed too much of the burden on our listeners to understand us and have assumed too little responsibility to make ourselves understood.

The privileged position of English in international discourse has allowed us to be unconscious of the difficulties many non-native English speakers encounter when we speak. Too many of us wing our way through international communication situations on automatic pilot. We speak too fast. We fling idiomatic phrases at our listeners. We concoct complicated sentences. We indulge in aimless digressions that frustrate and confuse. We imprecisely pronounce some of our words and swallow others. We just assume we will be understood,

This behavior sometimes impresses our international colleagues as arrogance, but I believe it is the fruit of circumstance. We have fallen prey to a sort of "linguistic Darwinism" in the sense that we are losing our capacity to adapt because we are accustomed to the world adapting to us. In short, our laziness and insensitivity spring from habit rather than arrogance, but since the impression of arrogance and disregard often prevails, not only do we fail to make our words understood but we also sabotage any feeling of goodwill that might miraculously sneak over, around, or through the language barrier.

Since the source of communication failures in international situations has been stood on its head, the common response to solving it, that is, "Let's give the non-native speakers a few hundred hours more of English lessons," hasn't resulted in tangle-free communications. Therefore, this book is about communicating effectively in English in an international environment. I wrote it to make native English speakers more aware of what we must do to help non-native English speakers understand us. I wrote it as a gift of respect for my European business and professional clients who have had to assume a disproportionate share of responsibility for each flawed communication between themselves and native English speakers.

It teaches us to "start where the international audience is." This focus is the pivotal difference between *The Global Speaker* and other books on public speaking, because understanding and responding to the different way the non-native audience listens is the key to bridging the gap between simply going through the motions of a presentation and communicating.

It is a book in cross-lingual communication where the word *cross-lingual* defines a situation in which the speaker is mother-tongue English but all or most of the audience is not. Throughout this book, I use the term *cross-lingual* to define this audience. I use the term *native* to delineate the mother-tongue speaker of English and *non-native* to describe the non–mother-tongue speaker of English.

This book is in the form of a primer because it outlines the first principles of making successful international presentations. Most of these principles will help us to be better communicators in Rome, New York, as well as Rome, Italy, but because we are approaching the issue of communication from the perspective of a native English speaker talking to a non-native speaker, everything we may have previously learned from books or seminars about successful presentations will be viewed from a different angle. Some techniques that are incidental when speaking to an audience of native speakers will acquire a special emphasis when addressing a cross-lingual audience.

This is a short book because it assumes we are going to be making an international presentation and will want to spend more time developing the presentation and preparing ourselves to deliver it and less time reading a book about it. It is a handbook, not a textbook, to be consulted whenever we are preparing a presentation for an international audience. Because it is a handbook rather than a textbook, its value lies not in reading and knowing the principles outlined but in practicing them. Reading the book ten times won't be as valuable as applying its principles one time.

What follows is as much a journey in consciousness-raising as it is a primer of presentation techniques. It is so much a compendium of common sense that we might wonder why it was written at all, but it was written because common sense is often a rare visitor in speaking situations, especially international ones. We frequently hide our nerves behind distracting habits and mannerisms. We easily clothe ourselves in the security blanket of our mother tongue whose words we can ramble effortlessly without sufficient attention to clarity. We often become so thoroughly lost in ourselves and our content that both we and our content are lost on our audience.

A word about what this book is not. It is not a book on cross-cultural communication in the sense of pinpointing cultural traditions that make doing business in Saudi Arabia different from doing business in Indonesia. It doesn't address such issues as whether we should bow, shake hands, or simply nod when we are introduced. This is not because I consider knowledge of the cultural traditions of our host country unimportant but only because it lies beyond the scope of this book.

In the final analysis, all effective communication begins with attitude—a genuine desire to understand and to make ourselves understood. For the native English speaker in the international arena, this means "starting where the audience is," which includes a respect for the cross-lingual audience's willingness to communicate in our language, an appreciation of the effort their willingness entails, and finally, a corresponding effort on our part to be as clear and comprehensible as possible. The suggestions that follow are in the form of rules or guidelines. They are really a checklist designed to put us in the place of our audiences so that we can better serve their needs, which in the end will also serve our own.

Whenever we have an international encounter, it is wise to remember that we may be the guests geographically, but we are the hosts linguistically. We may be standing or sitting around other people's tables, eating from their china, but all the food for thought will be cooked and served in English, our language. Whether the meal is a success, whether what we serve is swallowed and digested, left on the plate and rejected, or simply sits badly and leaves an unpleasant taste in the mouth, depends largely on us.

I expect the day is drawing nearer when increasing numbers of native English speakers will have to learn other languages, and English may, in time, cede its position as the international language as other languages have before it. In the interim, our work, as the natural heirs of English, is to communicate more clearly and sensitively in our own mother tongue.

2

Structure: Creating and Maintaining Context

An executive from a large U.S. chemical company was addressing a group of international managers on "The High Cost of Industrial Accidents." As he reeled off the human, environmental, and financial toll of disasters, such as Bhopal, he was surprised to observe in his audience a sea of tightly grinning faces. He gradually made peace with his discomfort by telling himself that the disconcerting smiles were expressions of agreement with his comments. His discomfort returned at the end of his presentation, however, when he was met with a disquieting silence. There were no questions or remarks from the audience, only a polite thank-you from the meeting chair. Hadn't he gotten through to them? Weren't they interested? They had certainly looked interested, even receptive. "What happened?" he asked me later in relating his sense of failure. "I wasn't there, so I can only speculate," I said, "but from your description, I would say that what you mistook for inappropriate grins or receptive smiles may have been their ears squinting." What did I mean?

In my early efforts to understand a foreign language, I became aware of a facial tension that felt similar to how we squint our eyes when we are trying to see something in the distance or to distinguish something that is not clear. This "squinting of the ears" manifests itself in a tensing of the jaw muscles and often takes the form of a broad, tightly held grin. In international meetings, speakers often misread this expression as receptivity to, or agreement with, our comments.

I have an amusing collection of anecdotes from my first months in Europe. I began to notice how frequently business and professional people selected me out of a group, unwittingly ignoring the others, and directed their comments exclusively to me. At first I thought there was something embarrassingly askew in my appearance—an unbuttoned blouse or spinach lodged in my teeth. Then I thought it was because I was a foreigner. I soon realized that they focused on me because I was poised on the edge of my chair gazing intently at them with what seemed to be an accommodating smile on my face. Instead, my ears were squinting in a colossal effort to understand. Most probably, my comprehension rate was about one-third that of my native-language colleagues who were peering out the window or admiring the paintings on the walls.

Listening in our mother tongue is a relatively relaxed experience. It feels effortless. Vast experience with our own language allows us to immediately recognize the words in a sentence that carry meaning, in much the same way as a seasoned gatherer can venture into the woods and expertly know which plants are edible and which are poisonous. Often, we can even fill in the blanks if we do not hear every word in a sentence. Non-native English speakers, on the other hand, are often still mastering vocabulary and the patterns of phonology, grammar, and syntax that come casually to us. We can successfully eavesdrop on conversations we overhear in a restaurant, on a bus, or while walking down the street, and understand them, even though the conversations are not directed to us. Non-native English speakers need an elevated comprehension level to engage in eavesdropping.

For many of the people we will be speaking to in international meetings, listening is an active event rather than a passive event. They must listen with highly focused attention, selecting the salient items of each sentence and then retaining these items so that they can make sense of the overall communication. It is a stressful and even exhausting process made more difficult because, unlike the written word, where several drafts and a good proofreader produce sentences that are carefully structured and ordered, speech is often characterized by incomplete sentences, lengthy digressions, false starts, and jerky transitions.

Context is the wedding between language and situation. It is the key to comprehension. Well-trained foreign-language instructors teach new vocabulary by presenting it in a contextual framework. For example, the word *fire* may be taught in the context of the "language of cooking" (making a fire/lighting a fire), or it may be taught in the context of the "language of personnel management" (to fire an employee). Both the meaning of the word and its grammatical function (in the first instance a noun, in the second a verb) change depending on the context. This contextual alteration of word meaning is especially peculiar to English. As only one example, note the various contextual meanings of the word *bear*.

He saw a bear in the woods.
He can't bear the suspense any longer.
She's bearing up pretty well.
Will you bear witness to this event?

In addition, two English words can have the same pronunciation but a different spelling and meaning, as in, for example, "Give me the bare facts." And then there are those words that are spelled alike but have different pronunciations and meanings. When I began to teach English as a foreign language, many clients expressed their frustration that we wind a watch with a long i, but the wind blows with a short i. When Pavarotti comes to town for a concert, they want to know why he sings live with a long i, in the city where they live with a short i. As native English speakers, we take these linguistic circumstances so much for granted that we do not even notice them. They are definitely hurdles for the cross-lingual audience, however, so it is incumbent on us as owners of the language to provide a context that either removes these hurdles, or at least enables the cross-lingual audience to leap over them.

After attending a meeting or a conference in English, my clients would often complain that they missed large portions of a speaker's comments because they "had lost the context." Either the speaker failed to establish a strong context at the outset, or was unable to maintain it due to digressions and abrupt topic changes. The failure to establish and maintain context stems from our own lack of clarity about our subject, or from faulty organization of our ideas. If we ramble our way through an international presentation, chances are that this is our habit in all presentation situations, but the consequences are not the same with a cross-lingual versus a native-English-speaking audience. Mother-tongue English speakers are better able to follow our side trips because English is their turf.

If someone takes us on a roundabout journey through our own hometown, we might be irritated by unnecessary detours down side streets and back alleys, but we will probably recognize enough landmarks along the way to feel secure that should we end up in a strange neighborhood, we can eventually find our way home. Non-native English speakers are linguistically akin to visitors in a strange city with only a tourist map to guide them. Should we lure them away from the center and off the map, they are lost. They have no familiar landmarks or signposts to orient them. As speakers, we must map out a clear route for the non-native English speaker and stay within the confines of it. Linguistically, mapping out a clear route means structuring our presentation so that it establishes and maintains context.

Certainly there are a host of methods for organizing a presentation. Of the many systems to which I have been exposed, I personally recommend the Decker Grid System™ developed by Decker Communications, Inc., as an example of an excellent way to put together a presentation that creates and maintains context for the cross-lingual audience. It has the additional advantage of reducing the amount of time required to organize a presentation, which will give us more time to rehearse and to attend to the other considerations discussed in this book.

The following is an adaptation of the Decker Grid System™ and how to use it. Under each step, I include commentary on the relevance of each point for the cross-lingual audience. The accompanying diagrams visually summarize the system so that a glance at them is all that will be necessary to reference the system for future organizational use.

To begin we simply require (1) a clear desk or work surface, (2) a pad of Post-it™ notes (1 1/2 x 2 inches), and (3) our ideas. The grid is divided into four parts:

1. Laying the *Cornerstones*
2. *Brainstorming* for ideas
3. *Clustering* ideas
4. *Composing* the presentation

Before we begin with the first part of the process, we need to be acquainted with note concepts. A **note concept** is a symbol or one to four words representing an idea that it would take several sentences or paragraphs to elaborate if we were writing it out word-forword. Since each idea or thought is briefly captured on a separate Post-it, using note concepts is the first step toward creating and maintaining context. Using note concepts breaks us of the habit of writing out sentences and paragraphs before we have clearly organized our ideas. Although it is possible to use the backs of business cards, 3-by-5 inch cards, or separate slips of paper for this process, Post-its have two distinct advantages. First, they are small, so we cannot be tempted to write too much on them. Second, they are mobile. We often change our minds about the order of things. If we outline our speech on a piece of paper, we inevitably end up crossing out lines, drawing arrows, and scribbling in the margins. The result is an outline that resembles a poor imitation of a Jackson Pollack painting. We have to copy it over and frequently change our minds again.

With Post-its, it is simple to change order and to add or delete ideas.

Laying the Cornerstones

Just as cornerstones set the foundation of a building, the cornerstones of a presentation establish its foundation. Strong, well-articulated cornerstones create a clear context for our cross-lingual audience.

State the Subject

Before we actually lay the cornerstones of a structure, it is necessary to decide whether we are building a geodesic dome, a conventional two-bedroom one-story house, or a fifty-floor skyscraper. In the framework of a presentation, this means starting with a well-modeled subject. I consulted once with a lawyer who was to give a presentation at an annual meeting of her state's bar association. When asked the subject of her speech, this is what she said:

> I'm going to talk about why it should be illegal for the media to publish any information on a criminal case until the accused has been tried and a verdict has been handed down because otherwise the press coverage could interfere with the possibility of selecting a jury and it could prejudice the client's right to a fair trial, as well as the prosecutor's ability to use certain evidence.

This explanation was not the subject. Rather, it encompassed several of the major points she wanted to argue in her speech. Quite simply, the subject of her speech was "Criminal Law and the Media." A subject is neutral and to the point. It should not be confused with a title, which can be longer, opinionated, and cleverly stated. The title serves to attract audience interest. The subject statement is primarily for us. It helps us begin the process of sculpting the subject. The cornerstones we lay are even more specific and put boundaries around our subject. (See Diagram 1.)

Establish a Point of View on the Subject

Our point of view (POV) is our opinion, attitude, or position on the subject. It is an integral part of our relationship to the subject. One of the best ways to isolate our point of view is to ask the question "So what?" or "Who cares?" in relation to our subject. The answer is our POV. The subject, "Criminal Law and the Media," could go in many directions. It is our point of view that determines the direction. The following are examples of concise, unambiguous points of view.

Example 1:

Subject: The Unified European Market

POV: The Unified European Market gives us an unparalleled opportunity to expand our company's international presence.

Example 2:

Subject: Criminal Law and the Media

POV: The media should be prohibited from pub-

Diagram 1.   Cornerstones (outline).

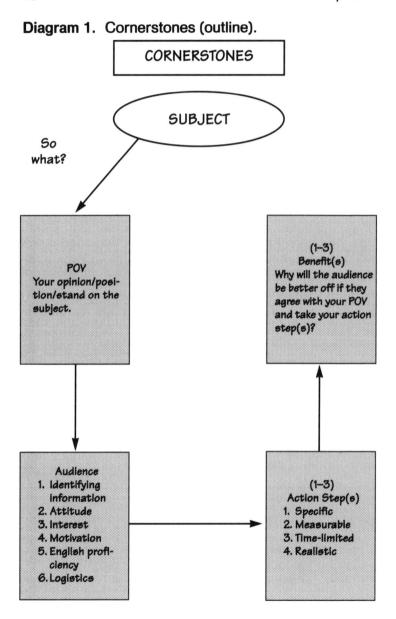

lishing preverdict information in criminal cases.

Besides helping us to be lucid about our subject, a concisely articulated POV acts as a rudder that steers the listening of our cross-lingual audience. When we give the audience an immediate and unambiguous declaration of our position on the subject, we create the context from which our arguments will follow. The audience listens to everything we have to say in terms of how it does or does not support our point of view. As a result, our point of view should be stated early in our presentation and not at the end. A speech is not a detective story in which the audience much search for clues and guess the motive and the outcome. A cross-lingual audience is more than sufficiently challenged by the non-native language and the inevitable twists and turns delivered by different speakers. Additional mystery will not be welcomed. Nor does it serve us or our cross-lingual audience if we assume that it is improper to have and state a point of view. We always have a POV when we speak but often we are foggy about it, timid to own it, or inept at stating it. To make the cross-lingual audience responsible to fish a POV out of a bucket of information and data shortchanges both the audience and ourselves.

In my seminars on communicating with clarity, whenever a participant completes a presentation, I ask the other participants to give a one-sentence feedback statement of the speaker's point of view. On the first morning of the seminar before we have worked on establishing and articulating strong POVs, it is common for each speaker to receive as many versions of his or her point of view as there are participants in the seminar. Often none of the perceived POVs matches the intention of the speaker. Obviously, this is derailed communication, and we are surprised by it. We like to believe that we communicate more lucidly than we actually do. When this lack of clarity is so pervasive in native language situations, we can only imagine how severely the problem is compounded in a cross-lingual one.

Ironically, non-native English speakers who have studied business and professional English learn to recognize and make clear opinion statements, and they are bewitched, bothered, and bewildered when native English speakers do not live up to the EFL (English as a foreign language) textbooks.

Analyze the Audience

The underlying premise of this book is that we must start where the audience is. It is the result of analyzing one aspect of the cross-lingual audience, that is, how the non-native language changes the international communicating environment for the audience and for us. We must analyze our particular audience even further if we are to "start where the audience is" in relationship to our subject. Our interest and enthusiasm in our topic, though necessary, are not sufficient to interest and enthuse our listeners. We need to lock into their interests and enthusiasms.

The following points are areas we would do well to explore to have a better understanding of our prospective audience. To do this analysis, we must draw on previous experience, as well as ask questions of our colleagues and our host or liaison person. Where information is not available, we may choose to follow some hunches, knowing that we must remain open and flexible to shift gears should we find in the midst of the presentation that our information or intuition has proved to be misguided.

We should pose the following questions to ourselves before putting together the presentation, noting the answers to each question on a Post-it. We will not be able to answer all the questions, and we may find some of them irrelevant. We should, however, prepare a Post-it with a question mark for any specific information we feel we must have about the audience. We can then set about getting this information.

Who Are They?

Are they peers, superiors, or subordinates? What are their positions? What is their decision-making capacity? Is there any other identifying information (gender, race, ethnicity, age, income, education, etc.) that is relevant to selecting the data we will use to present our points?

For example, in giving a speech titled "Sexual Harassment," the gender makeup of the audience might not affect our POV, but the data and examples we use to elaborate our points might vary because the genders might view the subject differently.

How Do They Feel About Us and Who We Represent?

Is there any previous history that would predispose the audience to be welcoming or not welcoming? Have we already established a relationship with the audience or is this our first encounter?

What Is Their Interest in and Knowledge of Our Subject?

Why are they present? What is their interest in the subject? Are they enthusiastic about it? Bored? Indifferent? Is it controversial? How well-informed are they?

What Is Their Attitude Toward Our Point of View?

Do they support it? Oppose it? Are they skeptical about it? Have no established opinion about it?

What Motivates Them?

Are they interested in efficiency? Economy? Power? Prestige? Social change? Justice? Equality? Due process? Academic integrity? Personal development? The possibilities are legion, but usually a group is clustered around a certain set of shared values and goals with some variations within subgroups. For example, bank branch managers may put a high value on good customer service and efficiency, whereas the bank tellers may be more motivated by less stressful work conditions and higher salaries. The range of needs must be taken into consideration when we address a mixed group.

What Is Their English-Language Proficiency?

It is relatively uncomplicated to find out the language composition of a group in terms of whether they all speak the same language or whether it is an audience of many nationalities and mother tongues. Unfortunately, it may not be so simple to learn the fluency level of the group if we have not spoken to the group previously or have not had much prior contact by telephone or personal meeting. Non-native English speakers have a hard time evaluating their spoken fluency. They do not really know how they sound in a foreign language. Generally, they are more secure in evaluating their comprehension level. They know whether they have understood or not, but even in this area so much depends on the native English speaker that uncertainty reigns.

Another reason why we may not know in advance the language level of our audience is that the company liaison might be vague or falsely reassuring and casually announce to us, "No problem. Everyone speaks English." In any case, there can be a wide range of fluency within a group. The best we can do is to ask more specific questions such as: How many in the group have attended presentations in English before? Were there any problems? What were they?

Attending meetings in English is routine for some, but only an occasional occupational event for many others. People love to swap "war stories" after a meeting about who and what they did not understand or misunderstood. Becoming privy to these anecdotes can be a valuable source of information for us.

It is customary for international guests to be squired about by a person or persons selected precisely because they speak excellent English. These people do such an exemplary job of making us feel at home that we often launch into our formal presentation as though we are, in fact, at home. The special language needs of our audience may vanish from our minds. We would do well, instead, to step outside the comfort zone provided by the liaison and find opportunities to immerse ourselves in the milieu of our target audience.

A reliable and available way to understand the language level of the audience is to mingle informally before the presentation. We can learn a great deal about a group by spending as little as ten minutes having coffee in the corridor with them. Who initiates and sustains conversation with us? Who avoids us? Are people able to respond to questions we ask? Do people quickly drift away from us and start a conversation in their native language? Granted, people may avoid us because they are timid or don't want to impose. They may misunderstand our question because they were distracted by another conversation. They may strike up a conversation in their own language because they need to communicate with a colleague at that moment, and they may suddenly drift away because our deodorant has failed. Nevertheless, we can get a reasonably accurate read on our prospective listeners that lets us know whether we need to slow our pace, repeat key concepts, or adjust ourselves in other ways to assist audience comprehension when we speak to the group formally. Mingling before the presentation is also a good way to establish rapport with the group.

When and Where Will We Be Speaking?

Presentation logistics are always important, but especially with cross-lingual audiences. Competing noises and activities are less disturbing to a native English audience than to a cross-lingual one. A room with many distractions, such as people wandering in and out, a telephone ringing, noise from surrounding rooms, or a loud heating or cooling system, imposes major problems. We should take responsibility to remove distractions when possible, or take steps to overcome them by speaking more loudly, moving closer to the audience, repeating some of our statements, or holding our comments until the disturbance abates.

Exactly when we speak also has an effect on the cross-lingual audience. For example, audience attention is generally lower after lunch. The body is focused on digesting food, not ideas. Similarly, if we speak at the end of the day after the audience has been sitting and listening to other speakers for a long time, we should not be surprised if their brains are as numb as their behinds. There are ways to rise above both instances. For example, we can have a stretch break before we begin. If we are the first presentation after lunch and expect to speak for more than half an hour, we should pause midway for a stretch break.

Finally, if we follow a speaker who has spoken in the native language of the audience, the audience may need time to switch channels and get into English. Clients have told me that they also need time to adjust to British English after hearing American English and vice versa, as they suffer a momentary comprehension warp. We can facilitate the transition by speaking more slowly and precisely and by extending the ice-breaking chatter before getting into the meat of our speech so that the audience can become familiar with our way of speaking.

Specify an Action Step(s) for the Audience to Take

At this moment, I am inputting these words into my computer. I am giving it information. If I do not give the computer a command telling it what I want it to do with this information (e.g., Save it! Print it! Link it! Copy it!), the information will be lost when I turn off the computer. According to the axioms of pragmatic communication, each communication consists of a report that is the content of the message and a command that indicates how the message is to be taken.

Though some of us will acknowledge that we speak with the objective of inspiring or motivating our listeners, more of us would insist that all we are doing is giving a report, supplying information, summarizing proceedings, or presenting research findings. Many of us might be resistant to the idea of incorporating a request for action into our presentations. Yet, whether our purpose is to report, to inform, or to summarize, we are giving our audience this information because we want them to do something with it. If our goal is to motivate or to inspire, we are motivating or inspiring them to *do* something. This message should not be left unstated or vague.

An **action step** is especially pertinent for the cross-lingual audience because it is explicit. Implications can be lost on the cross-lingual audience, as they require the audience to be attuned to nuances and subtleties. Most non-native English speakers are too busy attending to the spoken lines to try and fathom what is unspoken between the lines.

Foreign-language instructors teach listening comprehension by posing specific questions before the listening exercise. By asking the students to listen for specific things, the listening task is organized. Telling the audience what we expect at the outset of our presentation serves a similar purpose and increases attention, retention, and comprehension.

An effective action step is (1) specific, (2) measurable, (3) time limited, and (4) realistic. Our audience knows what we want from our listeners and the results can be measured; the time in which it must be done is clear; and what we are asking is realistic in that it is within the power of the audience to do what we ask. The action step is a barometer that lets us know how well we have succeeded with the cross-lingual audience. Without the action step, we may wallow in "maybe land" for months, thinking we have achieved commitment when we have not.

Example 1:

Subject: The Unified European Market

POV: The Unified European Market gives us an unparalleled opportunity to expand our company's international presence.

Audience: Upper Management XYZ Corporation

Action: 1. Draw up expansion plan within sixty days.
2. Arrange bank financing.

Example 2:

Subject: Criminal Law and the Media

POV: The media should be prohibited from publishing preverdict information in criminal cases.

Audience: State Bar Association

Action: 1. Establish a task force at this conference.
2. Draft a position paper within two months.

Example 3:

Subject: A New EDP System

POV: We must install the new system within six months or our distribution network will collapse.

Audience: EDP Support Staff

Action: 1. Work overtime for two months.
              2. Reschedule vacations.

Identify and State the Benefits to the Audience of Taking the Action Step(s)

Even if we make a strong intellectual argument, people will not necessarily be convinced that it is in their interest to follow the recommendations we suggest. We could say that a strong intellectual argument needs to include personal advantage. This does not mean that everyone is slavishly self-serving. Rather, it means that people act out of their value systems. A well-worn adage in sales is "People buy on emotion and rationalize with fact." Ideas are products of the mind. We speak to people because we want them to consider, share, act upon, or contribute to our ideas. Although we may wish that ideas exist in an objective realm untainted by emotion, both history and science deny this wish. Just as quantum theory asserts that perception is not independent from the perceiver, an idea does not exist separately from the person who expresses it and the person to whom it is communicated.

One of the reasons for addressing motivation when we analyze the audience is that it forces us to make certain that benefits correspond to the needs and values of the audience. As with all aspects of our communication with the cross-lingual audience, benefits should be made explicit. They are the *why* that logically evolves out of the *what* of the action step(s).

Example 1:

Subject: The Unified European Market

POV: The Unified European Market gives us an unparalleled opportunity to expand our company's international presence.

Audience: Upper Management XYZ Corporation

Action: 1. Draw up an expansion plan within sixty days.
2. Arrange bank financing.

Benefits: 1. Higher visibility
2. Reduced production costs
3. Better distribution network.
(See Diagram 2.)

Example 2:

Subject: Criminal Law and the Media

POV: The media should be prohibited from publishing preverdict information in criminal cases.

Audience: State Bar Association

Action: 1. Establish a task force at this conference.
2. Draft a position paper within two months.

Benefits: 1. Greater influence
2. Enhanced protection of client–lawyer relationship
3. Less media pressure

Example 3:

Subject: A New EDP System

POV: We must install the new system within six months or our distribution network will collapse.

Audience: EDP Support Staff

Diagram 2. Cornerstones (example).

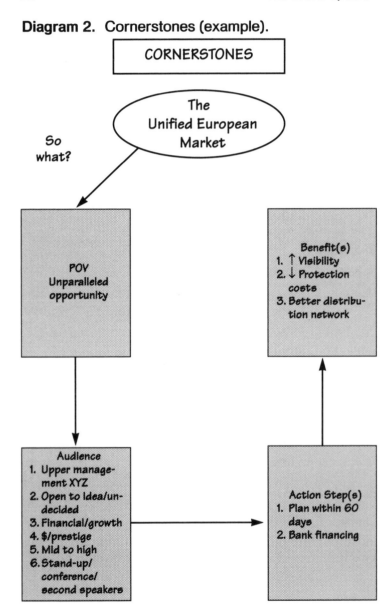

Action: 1. Work overtime for two months.
2. Reschedule vacations.

Benefits: 1. Overtime pay
2. Vacation bonus
3. Reduced workload once system is installed

Brainstorming

Badly structured presentations are usually the result of trying to organize our ideas prematurely. The solution is to empty our minds of all ideas about our subject before beginning to outline or organize the presentation. We would never try to paint a room and scrape the floors without first removing the furniture and taking the pictures off the walls, yet we commonly set out to organize presentations while all our ideas are still cluttered together. **Brainstorming** allows all of our ideas on a subject to flow without the interruption of prematurely trying to organize our thoughts. This saves time and enhances our creativity. The result is a greater wealth of ideas and organizational clarity. It is an important step in creating and maintaining context. The following are guidelines for brainstorming.

1. *Review the cornerstones to focus the mind.*
2. *Set a time limit.* It is a brainstorming exercise, not a soft summer breeze. Parkinson's Law, "The job expands to fill the time," is applicable to the organizational process. Setting a time limit puts the mind in gear and starts it moving.
3. *Capture each separate idea on a Post-it.* Two ideas that flow successively in brainstorming may not follow one another in the presentation.

4. *Place the ideas on Post-its randomly on the work surface.* Trying to organize each idea as it comes will interrupt the creative flow. Organization comes later.
5. *Do not censor any idea.* We need to suspend judgment at this point in the organizational process, as it is too early to decide what is relevant.
6. *Include anecdotes, stories, examples, and analogies.* We tend to censor these as though they were "soft" data and not significantly professional, academic, or scientific. In fact, they are what our audience remembers most from a presentation and can be used effectively to make points. They are highly recommended for a cross-cultural audience as long as they are not bound exclusively to our culture.

Clustering

Clustering is a preliminary organization of the ideas that we have brainstormed.

1. *Survey the Post-its and cluster them into groups according to ideas that seem to be talking about or elaborating the same point.*
2. *Put each cluster in a separate area of the work surface.*
3. *Select a title for each cluster that best describes what key point of our presentation the cluster is explaining or developing.*
4. *Each cluster title becomes a key point in our presentation.*

> *Example Subject: The Company Security System*
>
> *Key Point 1:* Define the problem.
> *Key Point 2:* Give the background of the
> problem.
> *Key Point 3:* Explain the proposed solutions.
> *Key Point 4:* Provide recommendations.

5. *Post-its under each cluster are the subpoints of the key point that the cluster represents.*
6. *Note that some clusters may be irrelevant and will be eliminated.* Others may be important but "slender," and we will need to brainstorm more to "fatten them up."
7. *Try to consolidate key points so that they do not exceed four.*

Communications research holds that the number of key ideas the human mind can retain at any one time is seven, plus or minus two, depending on the complexity of the material and other factors. For the cross-lingual audience, it is best to limit the key points to three or four. It is better to analyze the material and find a way to consolidate it into fewer points than to have a laundry list that may intimidate our audience. Making deep grooves on a few essential points is preferable to briskly skating over too many.

Composing the Presentation

Serviceable advice for effective presentations is: *Tell them what you're going to tell them. Tell them. Tell them what you've told them.* This advice can be multiplied tenfold for the cross-lingual audience. It tersely summarizes the structure necessary to create and maintain context. In order to follow this time-honored adage, we need to create the body of our presentation before we compose the opening and the closing. (See Diagram 3.)

The body is the key points plus the subpoints. The body of the presentation is composed of the key points derived from our clusters. Each cluster is a key point. The data that resulted from the brainstorm that elaborates each cluster are the subpoints. They are usually statistics, statements, examples, anecdotes, and quotes that support and amplify our argument. We should review them and place them in the order that we want to talk about them.

Ice-breaking comments to establish rapport. The audience need some settling-in time and so do we. Cross-lingual audiences need to become accustomed to our voice, accent, and pace of speaking, and it is wise to give them this time before we launch into the heart of our presentation. Comments about the country we are in, our trip, the hospitality of our hosts, or even better, a reference to a shared experience, can relax us and prime the group for our presentation.

The opening should include the following items:

- *An attention-getting opening.* A short anecdote, a strong POV statement, a quote, or rhetorical questions command attention. We must be careful that the anecdote is not too long or the quote linguistically archaic or too complicated. We should use rhetorical questions with a cross-lingual audience as opposed to questions requiring a show of hands or a vocal response. The introduction to a speech is too early to demand participation from a cross-lingual audience who need to

Diagram 3. Speech composition outline.

Composing

1. Select the 3 most important key points and prioritize.
2. Cluster the 3 most important subpoints under each key point.
3. Create the opening and closing. (Consolidate all action steps on one Post-it™ and all benefits on one Post-it™ if they are part of the opening and/or closing.)

Opening

1. Gain attention (e.g., quotation, story, questions, POV, strong statement).
2. State POV.
3. Self-introduction (if not formally introduced).
4. Transition to body of talk (e.g., action step(s), benefit(s), preview of key points).

Key Point 1
Main arguments to gain understanding/agreement with the POV or persuade to take action step(s)

Key Point 2

Key Point 3

Sub Point 1
Develop key points using
1. Stories
2. Analogies
3. Quotations
4. Data/Statistics
5. Examples

Subpoint 1

Subpoint 1

Subpoint 2

Subpoint 2

Subpoint 2

Subpoint 3

Subpoint 3

Subpoint 3

Closing

1. Summarize POV, action step(s), benefits or key points.
2. End with impact (e.g., quotation, success story, emotional plea, answer to a self-imposed question, a call to action).

get used to us first. We should avoid jokes as openers, as few people tell them well, often they are irrelevant, sometimes they are offensive, and customarily they are culture bound and do not cross the language barrier well.

- *A statement of the point of view.* The point of view is our major contextual statement and should be made concisely within the first minute of the presentation.
- *A statement of the action step(s) and benefits.* In a native-language situation, we might choose to state the action step and benefits at the end of our argument. With cross-lingual audiences, it is valuable to state them before getting into our key points and subpoints, and to repeat them again after we have argued our points. The benefits of doing this are setting context, focusing listening, and reinforcing retention. This opening structure leaves no surprises, but it gives the cross-lingual audience a sturdy strap to hang onto as they listen to the body of the presentation. The nicest surprise we can give them is the opportunity to leave our presentation feeling that they have understood a native English speaker better than they ever dreamed possible.
- *A preview of the key points and a transition into the presentation.* Example: "I'll be talking about four things. First, the definition of the problem; second, the background of the problem; third, some proposed solutions; and finally, my recommendations. First, what is the problem?"

An effective closing is a summary. People remember best what they hear last. Therefore, a good summary can briefly recap the point of view, the action step(s) and benefits, and possibly the key points. Repetition is an oratorical tool that promotes clarity and retention. It is an asset to any presentation and a necessity in cross-lingual presentations. A native English speaker may need to hear something more than once for emphasis and impact. A non-native English speaker often needs to hear important information more than once for comprehension. Moreover, summarizing the presentation also positions our key ideas in the forefront of our listeners' minds.

Once we have used this system or some variation that promises an equal measure of attention to creating and maintaining context, we should rehearse it several times to achieve crispness of structure and flow of ideas. Walking through our presentation several times will ensure that we do not allow a strong structure to slip into a sloppy one. I recommend "speaking the outline"—a technique I have used successfully in seminars. It requires us to cite only the major parts of the opening, body, and closing.

Using our first example, look at the notes and then follow how the main pillars of the presentation can be stated in less than two minutes, leaving us the rest of our allotted time to put the flesh on a well-formed skeleton.

Subject: The Unified European Market

    I. Opening
       a. *Attention Getter:* EC-92 motor oil
       b. *POV:* Unparalleled opportunity

  c. *Action:*
   (1) Draw up an expansion plan within sixty
    days.
   (2) Arrange bank financing.
  d. *Benefits:*
   (1) Higher visibility
   (2) Reduced production costs
   (3) Better distribution network
  e. *Preview:*
   (1) Unification background
   (2) Company situation
   (3) Opportunities
   (4) Benefits

 II. Body
  a. Unification background
  b. Company situation
  c. Opportunities
  d. Benefits

 III. Closing
  a. *POV:* Unparalleled opportunity
  b. *Benefits:*
   (1) Higher visibility
   (2) Reduced production costs
   (3) Better distribution network
  c. *Action:*
   (1) Draw up an expansion plan within sixty
    days.
   (2) Arrange bank financing.

  The "talking of the outline" might go something
like this:

Attention Getter:

Some people think that EC-92 is a new motor oil, but you and I know that it is the symbol for the economic and political unification of Western Europe whose target date was 1992.

POV:

I am convinced that this event offers our company an unparalleled opportunity to expand our international presence.

Action:

After I have explained the situation and opportunities to you in greater depth, I hope you will agree to draw up an expansion plan within the next sixty days and arrange for bank financing of the plant.

Benefits:

If we take these actions we will provide our company with higher visibility, lower production costs, and a better distribution network.

Preview:

For the next twenty minutes, I'd like to discuss in greater detail with you the background issues surrounding European unification, our current company situation, the opportunities in Spain, and the benefits of expanding into the European market.
First, European unification . . .
Second, our company situation . . .
Third, the opportunities in Spain . . .
Finally, the benefits of expansion . . .

Closing:

In closing, I would like to repeat that I think the unification of Western Europe in 1992 has given us an unparalleled opportunity to expand our interna-

Diagram 4. Example of the completed speech with Post-it™ notes.

Attention Getter EC = 92 Motor oil	POV Unparalleled opportunity	Action 1. Plan within 60 days 2. Bank financing Benefits 1. ↑ Visibility 2. ↓ Production costs 3. Distribution network	Preview 1. Background 2. Company situation 3. Opportunities and benefits

BACKGROUND	COMPANY SITUATION	OPPORTUNITIES AND BENEFITS
History of EC	Financial	Why Spain? 1. Economics 2. Resources 3. Distribution 4. Labor
Economic Situation 1. Past 2. Present 3. Future	Personnel	Benefits 1. ↑ Visibility 2. ↓ Production costs 3. Better distribution network
Doing Business from Europe	Production Capabilities	Seizing Opportunity 1. Draw up plans within 60 days 2. Bank financing

POV Unparalleled opportunity	Benefits 1. ↑ Visibility 2. ↓ Production costs 3. Distribution network	Action 1. Draw up plan within 60 days 2. Bank financing

tional presence. As I have demonstrated in my remarks, it will give us higher visibility; it will reduce production costs; and it will give us a better distribution network. I urge you to develop a plan within the next sixty days to support this expansion and to arrange bank financing for the plant. Opportunity is more than knocking—it's nearly breaking the door down—and if we continue to turn a deaf ear, we could lose the chance to seize a great market opportunity. (See Diagram 4.)

The foregoing material is an example of how we can structure a presentation so that we create and maintain context for our cross-lingual audience. I do not hold that this is the only way to organize a presentation for the cross-lingual audience, but I strongly urge that we compare any system we are currently using to it. Once we are convinced that our structure creates context, we can shift our attention to the ways language can be used to maintain the context we have established and to ensure a higher level of comprehension and retention by the cross-lingual audience.

3

Language

A sturdy structure creates and maintains the context required by the cross-lingual audience to better understand and retain what we say, but it is not sufficient. A lucid structure must be supplemented by language that is at once precise, descriptive, and lively.

Words are the raw material of communication. We can use words to build a bridge that connects people or to construct a wall that divides them. The best way to build a communicative bridge is to keep our language simple. This does not mean resorting to a "Me Tarzan, you Jane" approach to speaking. Neither does it mean writing out the presentation word for word and then reading it. The ensuing boredom would hardly offset our painstaking efforts to choose the right words. Rather, simplicity means cultivating a sensitivity to specific words, phrases, and sentence structures as they may affect the non-native English speaker.

Achieving Language Simplicity

Use Headline Words and Phrases

The headline of a newspaper or magazine article announces, at a glance, the major theme of the article. A headline word or phrase in a presentation positions the main argument to be discussed. Headline words and phrases are essential for establishing and maintaining context.

Example:
"What are the benefits of adopting plan XYZ? As I see it, there are three benefits. The first benefit is . . ."

Be Consistent in the Repetition of Headline Words and Phrases

Variety of vocabulary adds spice when addressing an audience of native English speakers, but it can be the herb of confusion in a cross-lingual situation. Range and richness of vocabulary are a primary distinction between the native and non-native English speaker. Whereas the native speaker may know fifteen ways to express a single idea, the non-native speaker may have learned three to five. This accounts for one of the reasons that non-native English speakers with different mother tongues can frequently understand each other when they speak English. They are drawing from a smaller pool of words than most educated native English speakers. In addition, those who have studied English for business, professional, or scientific purposes are exposed to the same or similar English-language textbooks.

In order to maintain context and promote comprehension and retention, we should use the same headline word throughout the presentation and avoid synonyms. If we talk about *benefits*, we should not later refer to them as *advantages*.

Use Transition Words That Establish Sequence

Listening to a speech with jerky or nonexistent transitions is like trying to follow someone in a car who drives too fast, races through yellow lights, and makes abrupt turns without signaling. Inevitably, the follower gets lost. It is a great tactic if the driver is James Bond bent on shaking a tail. It is disastrous if the goal is to have the car in the rear arrive at the same destination as the lead car.

Transitions are the art by which one step in the evolution of thought arises out of another. Establishing the sequence of ideas creates an outline in the mind of the listener that focuses listening and increases retention. Equally important, it leads us away from the temptation to indulge in obfuscating digressions. Finally, transition words break the whole into its constituent parts, which enables a listener to comprehend more detail. We eat a steak by cutting it into pieces. Similarly, the best way for an audience to ingest a discourse is for us to feed it to them in bite-size pieces. A useful technique for establishing sequence is to use the *Tell them what you're going to tell them. Tell them. Tell them what you've told them* formula discussed in relationship to structuring content: *Explain to your listeners what you are going to tell them. Tell them what you promised. Summarize what you've told them.*

Example:
    "I would like to do three things: First, define the problem; second, examine the causes of the problem; and finally, explore some solutions to the problem. First, define the problem. The problem is . . . Second, causes. What are the causes of the problem? . . . And, third (or finally), solutions. How can we solve this problem? . . ."

Key transition words for establishing sequence are: *first(ly)*, *second(ly)*, *third(ly)*, *finally*, *next*, *now*, and *in addition*. There are more idiomatic ways to change the topic (e.g., "Now let's look at/turn to/switch to/move on to"). Omit these or use them sparingly. Although some non-native English speakers have been exposed to them, many have not. Any changes in direction should be signaled without ambiguity. The less idiomatic words are more reliable for this purpose.

Avoid Complex Sentence Structure

A myriad of dependent, coordinate, subordinate, or relative clauses makes sentences difficult to follow. Favor simple or compound sentences where the relationship between subject and predicate (noun and verb) is clear.

Example:
"The port-a-potty design for the city park system will be ready next week. I think it's a good one, and I'll welcome your comments and suggestions."

[instead of]

Example:
"The project about which I have just been speaking is nearing completion within the week at which time we'll be asking you for your opinions, which I hope will end up being favorable, as are mine."

Define Abstract, Nonspecific Terms

An abstract, nonspecific term is a word that won't stand on its own two feet with a cross-lingual audience without a clarifying phrase to support it. We may have trouble identifying these words and phrases in advance if we think that the United States is the center of the universe, and that everyone we meet in the international business and professional world will laugh at the same jokes that we do and simultaneously follow the same trends. For most of the world our *number crunchers* are still their *accountants*. This is only one example of the picturesque words that enter our work environment. Unfortunately, most of these words do not make the trip around the world before we replace them with a newer version.

For the most part, we can go a long way toward catching these words simply by being on guard. With our antennae raised, we should (1) look out for and eliminate these terms when we structure our presentation; (2) tape-record or videotape ourselves when we practice the presentation and listen for unclear, esoteric, trendy, or culturebound terms during the playback; and (3) pay attention to the expressions on the faces of the cross-lingual audience while we are giving the presentation. If more than one or two people are looking puzzled when we say something, a buzzer should go off in our brains that tells us that clarification is needed.

Example:
"I want to talk about personal impact. By personal impact, I mean the influence or effect your attitude and behavior have on other people."

Avoid Jargon and Acronyms

Jargon and acronyms are a form of spoken shorthand. They expedite communication within a group privy to the abbreviations used. They have exactly the opposite effect on those who aren't "in the know." The use of letters as a substitute for the words they represent is especially deadly with non-native speakers of English. First, the pronunciation of English vowels can cause momentary confusion. For example, the English letter *a* is often pronounced like the English letter *e* in some romance languages. Even though non-native speakers have learned the English alphabet and are aware of the difference, a brief taste of a letter while being fed the alphabet soup of an acronym may cause them to first visualize the letter in their native language. Also, each language has its own word order, which is different from the English word order. This changes the order of the acronymic letters. Out of habit, cross-lingual listeners may revert quite naturally to their native-language word order when given a series of letters outside the context of a word.

Example:
  The U.N. (The United Nations—English)
  ONU (l'organizzazione delle nazioni uniti—Italian)

Avoid Idioms

Idioms are the warp and woof of a shared language. We'd probably be hard-pressed to explain the meaning of these idiomatic phrases even to native English speakers. In a nutshell, we shouldn't use an idiom unless we can explain what it means. Ask fifty native English speakers for the gist of the idiom "hell-bent for leather," and we might get a congruence of meaning including fast, hurried, reckless, and determined. Ask the same fifty people for a literal translation or the etymology of the phrase, and we'd possibly get fifty different answers. Ask either task of the cross-lingual audience, and they would probably ask when we're breaking for lunch. Many idioms have a sister idiom in a foreign language, but idioms do not directly translate, so it is best to avoid them, or if we're hell-bent on using them, explain what they mean.

Example:
"We have no intention of jumping out of the frying pan into the fire. In other words, if we accept Mr. Lucifer's proposal, we'll exchange our current situation for one that promises to be even worse."

Avoid Anglo-Saxon Phrasal Verbs and Prepositional Verbs

A verb used with an adverb particle (e.g., bring up, turn down, put off) is a phrasal verb. Phrasal verbs rank among the most difficult aspects of the English language for the non-native speaker because the meaning of the phrasal verb often differs from the meanings of the two words taken separately. Even consulting a dictionary doesn't resolve the problem for the non-native speaker because many phrasal verbs change their meaning depending on context—for example, make up can mean (1) to design, (2) to tell a lie or fabricate a story, (3) to resume a relationship after a rupture, or (4) to apply cosmetics to the face. Most non-native speakers would have to have lived in an English-speaking country for an extensive period in order to pick up some of the idiomatic phrases that we sprinkle so generously throughout our conversations.

I had a client who sat through a two-hour meeting in which the speaker talked frequently about sticking to the plan. At the break, my client, a gracious host, had someone come in to wipe the conference table clean. He thought food or drink had been left on it and was sticking to the plan. He didn't need to feel embarrassed when he discovered the meaning of the phrasal verb. Several others in the group had been equally puzzled by the expression.

Phrasal prepositional verbs consist of three parts: a base verb, an adverb particle, and a preposition (e.g., to get on with, to put up with, to check up on). There is absolutely nothing wrong with Anglo-Saxon phrasal and prepositional verbs in a native-language situation. After all, English does have Anglo-Saxon roots. Our purpose, however, is not to celebrate a chauvinistic pride in the origins of our language nor to give an English lesson to our audience, even if we could. Our purpose is to communicate. To ask a non-native English speaker to master the difference between *get to, get down, get in, get out, get over, get through, get by, get on with, get after,* and so forth, and the way the same phrasal can change meaning with context, is asking a bit much. (In fact, *Webster's New World Dictionary* devotes over one and a half pages of print to the different meanings of *get.*) We should use synonymous verbs in place of the phrasals. If possible, it is good to use verbs with Latin roots because many foreign languages have been influenced by Latin.

Example:
"I would like you to review the proposal, examine the suggested price structure, write your recommendations, and return them to my office by Monday."

[instead of]

Example:
"Look over the proposal, check out the price structure,

jot down your comments, and drop them by my office by Monday."

Do Not Overuse Pronouns

Pronouns may be little words, but they are high curbs that trip up many a non-native English speaker, especially combined pronouns. Many languages, as noted before, do not have the same word order as English. Often the indirect object pronoun is expected before the subject and the verb rather than after. The ability to understand who gave what to whom when pronouns are used is often one of the hardest things for a non-native English speaker to master on the road to fluency. To facilitate listening and comprehension for the cross-lingual audience, we should use the noun instead of the pronoun unless to do so would sound awkward and ridiculous.

Example:
   "Leave the report with my associate, Jane, or give the report to another associate or secretary in my office."

[instead of]

Example:
   "I'd like you to leave it with her or whoever else is there to get it from you."

Examples and Analogies Indigenous to the Audience

One of the best ways to involve our listeners and help them to understand and remember what we have said is to use examples and analogies that correspond to their world. As adults, we process new information in terms of what we already know. The key word, however, for using analogies in international presentations is *indigenous*. Businesspeople love to use sport analogies, but comparing the new corporate plan to a baseball team, though it may play well in Japan where baseball is a national sport, will strike out rather than score in a country where baseball is not played. If we are going to be doing a lot of international presentations and have a penchant for sport analogies, it might serve us well to learn something about soccer if we are not already knowledgeable, as this is probably the most widely played team sport in the world.

Consult an EFL/ESL (English as a Foreign Language/English as a Second Language) Textbook

EFL/ESL books, especially those that teach the language of business or the language of meetings, are an indispensable source for those of us who will be working with some regularity in the international environment. (One such book is enough, and the bookseller should be able to recommend a good one.) Most people who learn English for business or professional use have been exposed to these texts. It is the best way for us to start where the audience is from the point of view of language. Browsing through these books will acquaint us with many of the words and phrases most commonly learned by non-native speakers. It can also help us refine our own English-language use.

4

Nonverbal Skills

When I was sixteen years old, I was a foreign exchange student in Japan. To say I knew only the rudiments of the Japanese language goes beyond stretching the truth. More accurately, I'm pushing it over the edge of a cliff. Given that we were bursting with youthful energy and enthusiasm, it was expected that those of us embarking on this cross-cultural journey would soak up the language soon enough. I had been in Japan only one week, however, and had not yet become a linguistic sponge when I met my fellow students at a Tokyo railway station prior to our departure on a ten-day tour of the country. In the excitement and confusion of the moment, I inadvertently entered railroad car 6 while my companions crushed into car 5. In the brief period it took to realize my isolation, the train separated between cars 5 and 6, and I found myself on a train high-speeding its way out of the station in the opposite direction of the train with my friends.

Sometime later (a few seconds short of eternity), I exited at the first stop with high hopes of finding a telephone or a cheery station master who would immediately place me on a train pointed in the right direction and ready to go. What I found was a small rural village with one unpaved street running through its truncated middle with shabby wooden huts straddling both sides. As I walked down the quiet deserted lane, I tried to quell my anxiety by fantasizing that I was Gary Cooper in *High Noon*, but I had no six-shooter, and even worse, I had no Japanese phrasebook. Slowly, like a row of candles being lit one at a time, the residents began to appear in the doorways. I stared into their open-mouthed, toothless curiosity, all the while kicking myself figuratively around the block for not having chosen a Spanish-speaking country for my foreign exchange experience, since I speak Spanish.

We spent long minutes sniffing each other out before the silence was broken. When it was, of course, we didn't understand one another—not verbally, that is. What followed was a nonverbal dance of at least one-half hour in which each of us exhausted a vast repertoire of prejudices, suppositions, defenses, and misunderstandings, but eventually there was goodwill. Through body language, facial expression, touch, and voice, we managed to embrace one another across history, culture, and language. A farmer drove me back to Tokyo (the next train out of the tiny village would not have arrived until midnight), and I somehow was able to do everything necessary to hook up with my group in Kyoto.

How many of us have had similar experiences either more or less dramatic? In the absence of a common verbal ground, we are able to tap into a vast stockpile of nonverbal skills to communicate when we have to. Even though we are not at the mercy of our nonverbal skills when we encounter a cross-lingual audience that knows English as a foreign language, we would seriously diminish our ability to communicate effectively if we opted to disregard the contribution of the nonverbal element.

How we physically hold ourselves, the ways we move, how we use our hands, our facial expressions, how we look at people, the sounds of our voices, and the pace at which we speak are all behaviors that help our audience pay attention to, understand, and recall our message, or cues that distract from, muddle, and block our message. Nonverbal communication is indispensable when one is addressing a cross-lingual audience.

The importance of nonverbal elements in the communication process is debatable only to the extent that experts disagree on the percentage value assigned to individual elements such as posture, movement, facial expression, gestures, and other behaviors in juxtaposition to the actual words or message delivered. It is increasingly rare to find someone who says that nonverbal factors have no value whatsoever. Others say, along with Ralph Waldo Emerson, "What you are speaks so loudly, I cannot hear what you say." Strict purveyors of information are wont to believe that because information has its own inherent value, how it is packaged or delivered has (or should have) little or nothing to do with how it is received. These people would encounter an argument going back as far as Aristotle, who declared in his essay on *Rhetoric:*

> Since the art of speech aims at producing judgments . . . the speaker must not only look to his words, to see they are cogent and convincing, he must also present himself as a certain kind of person and put those who judge him

> in a certain frame of mind. . . . For it makes all
> the difference to men's opinions whether they
> feel friendly or hostile, irritated or indulgent.

The manner in which seemingly cold, hard, scientific facts are presented has a substantial effect on whether the information is (1) listened to, (2) understood, (3) remembered, and (4) believed. How many times have we encountered speakers for the first time and been immediately ready to disagree with them because of the way they presented themselves, while other speakers created an environment where we were willing to hear them out as well as give them the benefit of the doubt?

Like it or not, in an international communication situation, audience members, to some extent, regard us as stereotypes until we emerge as individual personalities. In the absence of actual behavior to judge us by, audiences often hold tentative expectations of us based on the categories we represent to them. Unless we have a reputation that precedes us, people are inclined to think of us in relation to the person who held our position before, in relation to other people from our company, country, region, profession, sex, ethnicity, or whatever. The audience member who comes to a meeting devoid of some preconceived notions has not been born yet. Open-mindedness is a willingness to change preconceived notions, whereas not having any preconceived notions is more akin to empty-mindedness. The minute we appear, even before we say a word, people begin to form impressions of us and opinions about us. What we say and how we behave throughout our speech will reinforce, alter, or totally eradicate this first impression, and what we communicate nonverbally may outweigh what we say verbally.

The importance of nonverbal behavior is also reflected in the works of the child development specialist Jean Piaget, and the eminent psychoanalyst Erik Erikson, both of whom posited that a child's capacity to trust is established at a preverbal age. Therefore, as adults, whenever we encounter a new person or situation, the cues we access to decide whether or not we trust someone are not language related. We do not need to be professional psychologists to know that if a person says one thing and does something else, we believe the behavior, not the words. Though the meaning of a particular behavior may be open to interpretation, the behavior itself is verifiable in reality. Words are conceptual only. People can lie and sometimes do. People can be mistaken and often are. With behavior, *what you see is what you get.*

Many of us continue to conduct business as if communication were words and nothing more. Consequently, most of our speech preparation is spent culling data and organizing them in some fashion. Customarily, we pay little or no attention to the nonverbal aspects of conveying our information. Some of us have simply been unaware of the importance of delivery skills. Others of us have harbored a dangerous arrogance that assumes people who pay attention to delivery style are shuck-and-jive artists pandering to an overgrowing population of ninnies.

Since the mid-1980s, many large corporations have invested in communication skill-training programs for select employees to correct this learned imbalance between style and substance. They have begun to recognize that data, ideas, and products do not stand apart from the people that represent them. Nevertheless, many people still persist in the prejudice that seminars focusing on nonverbal behavior are charm schools that teach people to value style over substance. Of course, the issue is not an "either/or" matter, and fortunately we do not have to choose between saying something poignant poorly and saying something meaningless masterfully. The most effective communicators have something worth saying and say it well. Saying it well implies a well-honed combination of both verbal and nonverbal skills.

A major roadblock to effective nonverbal communication is that, for the most part, we are unaware of our behavior in presentation situations. We lack the eye to see ourselves as others see us. We often inhibit our natural expressiveness because our internalized image of how we come across combined with our idealized model of how we *should* come across is misinformed or distorted.

The best way to cultivate nonverbal behaviors that accurately express us and support our message is to first rehearse our presentation aloud several times so that we are secure in the flow of ideas. Second, we should videotape ourselves, if possible, and then view the videotape as though we were a member of our prospective audience. Things to look for are behaviors that disturb the eyes or ears of the audience and/or distract them from the message; behaviors that create an impression contrary to the one we want to convey to the audience, for example, nervousness, insincerity, arrogance, lack of conviction; or behaviors that look unnatural and staged. *A cautionary remark:* The purpose of a videotape review is to transcend the limitations and inhibitions borne of nervousness, defensiveness, or habit. Our goal is not to don a new suit of artificial behaviors to replace the old, but rather to be genuine.

We want to pay attention to how and what we communicate nonverbally because the cross-lingual audience is especially sensitive to our nonverbal messages, tuning in to them to provide additional information to grasp the meaning of words they may not have heard before. When we are lost in a foreign country, we may not understand the verbal directions of the person we ask to rescue us, but we know whether he or she is pointing right or left, to the road in front of us or to the one behind. We also know from the way people nonverbally interact with us whether they are happy to help us or irritated.

The communications expert Marshall McLuhan became identified with the statement, "The medium is the message." Whenever we speak, we are the medium of our message. The following material is a summary of the most common nonverbal behaviors with some recommendations on why and how to use them to the mutual advantage of the cross-lingual audience and ourselves.

Voice

Voice is the conduit for our words. It includes:

How loudly or softly we speak (*volume*)
How fast or slowly we speak (*pace*)
How clearly we speak (*enunciation* and *pronunciation*)
How expressively we speak (*variety* or *inflection*)

It also includes the *quality* of the voice, that is, whether the voice is rich, resonant, and pleasant to listen to, or whiny, raspy, harsh, and an assault on the ear. Obviously, it is an asset to have a beautiful speaking voice that attracts and holds attention, and it is a liability to have a voice that grates on people's nerves. A voice that represents one of these extremes can measurably add to or detract from our effectiveness with a cross-lingual audience.

Most voices, however, are unremarkable. They evoke neither rave reviews nor pan notices. For most of us, improving the quality of the voice is not a necessity. This is not the case with other aspects of voice production (i.e., volume, pace, enunciation, and inflection), which may be the most crucial nonverbal factors in a cross-lingual situation.

The development of proper volume, pace, enunciation, and inflection is not technically demanding, but it is mentally taxing. It requires (1) a finely tuned self-awareness of how we sound in relation to these elements, (2) a heightened sensitivity to the needs of the cross-lingual audience, and (3) a concentrated effort to break detrimental habits that impede our commitment to communicate.

If we are unable to videotape ourselves, we should certainly audiotape our presentations. We do not hear ourselves as other people hear us. As a rule, when we hear ourselves on audiotape for the first time, the sensation is, "I don't sound like that." We want to blame the distortion we hear on the tape recorder. In fact, the way we usually hear ourselves is the distortion. If we are to get an accurate reading of how we are heard by others, we must hear ourselves from the outside-in rather than from the inside-out. When we hear ourselves with the "outer ear" of the audience, we should evaluate the following items.

Volume

Aim the Voice at the Farthest Person in the Room

If the audience cannot hear us, everything else is moot. The ability to hear without straining acquires added importance with a cross-lingual audience. People already have the stress of listening intently due to the language difference. Making it difficult to hear is stress squared. It is unfair to the audience. An intimate tone is adequate in a seated presentation of one to four people. A stand-up presentation or a seated presentation around a large conference table demands a louder voice. We should project the voice without shouting or making the voice unnaturally high-pitched or strident. We can achieve this by:

1. Pausing frequently
2. Taking a deep abdominal breath while pausing
3. Letting our words ride atop the column of air we produce as we slowly exhale

Do Not Let the Volume of the Voice Drop at the Ends of Sentences

It is a common habit for speakers to start each sentence with a bang and end it with a whimper. This happens because we are unable to sustain our breath. Many of us breathe shallowly, hold the breath in the chest, and are forced to speak from a very short column of air. When we run out of breath, the ends of our sentences become mumbled, garbled, inaudible, or nonexistent. The energy to project our words has disappeared. Moreover, if we do not pause frequently enough to replenish our breath, we will put undue pressure on the throat, which can cause an unpleasant vocal production and, in some instances, hoarseness.

The most problematic effect of dropping the volume of the voice at the ends of sentences is that the cross-lingual audience may lose the final words of the sentences. This word loss adds up to a significant portion of our comments when it is allowed to accumulate over the entire course of the presentation.

Use Eye Communication to Get Audience Feedback on the Voice

If we are lucky, someone in the audience will tell us if we are not speaking loudly enough, but we should not rely on luck, as people often think it is their own personal problem. The best strategy to sidestep this pitfall is self-awareness. Videotaping or audiotaping is a way to develop an internal instrument that will signal us when we need to modulate vocal volume. Until we can trust the accuracy of this instrument, however, we can monitor ourselves by paying attention to the visual messages we get from the audience while we are speaking. If a significant number of people are tilting their heads and seem to be straining to hear, they probably are. Similarly, if many people are suddenly leaning back in obvious withdrawal, chances are we are talking too loudly.

Generally, when volume is a problem, speakers tend to be too quiet rather than too loud, although cross-lingual situations sometimes produce the opposite phenomenon. For some reason, many people respond to the comprehension difficulties of non-native English speakers by shouting as though the non-native English speaker were partially deaf. It is sufficient to be aware that the tendency to shout our way through a language barrier exists. A better tactic is to let our eyes tell us what our ears may be keeping secret.

Pacing

Pacing is the fine art of knowing when to slow down and when to speed up—where to pause and for how long. It is a skill that every professional and business speaker would do well to develop. In a monolingual speaking situation, it marks the difference between a highly professional effort and merely going through the motions. In a cross-lingual environment, it marks the difference between those who are understood and those who are not. If we announce to a native-English-speaking audience our intention to "Get around to it," and we run our words together without pause, they will understand us. The cross-lingual audience, on the other hand, may spend several minutes wondering what a "round tuit" is and if they have ever seen one. The following suggestions explain how to use the pause to improve pacing.

Pause as Punctuation to Avoid Spill-Over Words and Run-On Sentences

Thissentenceisdifficultenoughtomakesenseofwhen wetrytoreaditsoofcourseitisobviousthatlisteningtoitespeciallyinaforeignlanguagewouldbeimpossibleandIam sureweallagreeisn'tthatright? Spill-over words and run-on sentences occur when we drive our words too fast. We skid through conceptual intersections, and we race past verbal stop signs and traffic lights with little regard for our fellow travelers. Consequently, we cause massive traffic jams and often gridlock in the brains of our listeners. The major complaint of non-native English speakers is that most mother-tongue English speakers talk too fast. We are not unique. To a non-native ear, it seems that most mother-tongue speakers talk too rapidly. Just as young people making the transition from adolescence to their early twenties often remark on how much more intelligent their parents have become in the last several years, many non-native English speakers, as they become more competent in English, remark on how much more slowly their English-speaking friends have begun to talk. So the good news is that all those complaints that we talk too fast are not totally our fault. The bad news is that it does not get us off the hook.

We must bear in mind that usually our presentations are to groups where there is a wide range of fluency. Addressing ourselves to the lower levels of fluency is not overly patronizing to those whose comprehension skills are at a higher level. After all, if we speak more slowly, the most fluent can still understand us, but if we speak too fast, we will lose those whose comprehension level is not high. We must also be aware that many of us simply speak too fast even for a native-English-speaking audience. The problem can easily be remedied by pausing where we would use punctuation when we write. Read the following paragraph without punctuation, then read it again, pausing wherever there would be a comma, period, colon, or semicolon.

Example:
   "We are disturbed by the dramatic drop in market share
I expect it will have a negative effect on our stock dividend
this year I am certain that at the annual meeting next week
unless I am mistaken and I hope I am we will see an angry
group of shareholders possibly ripe for an approach a takeover bid that is from some raider who wants to profit from
what I believe is only a temporary condition."

We could certainly express the ideas in this paragraph in a less fractured way by paying attention to
some of the recommendations made earlier on language
use. I insist on this paragraph as an example, however,
as it is representative of the way many of us speak, and
because it illustrates how we can use the pause to bail
ourselves and our audience out of a linguistic tangle.
Notice how much clearer it becomes with the pause as
punctuation.

[Revised]:
   "We are disturbed by the dramatic drop in market
share. [pause] I expect it will have a negative effect on our
stock dividend this year. [pause] I am certain that at the annual meeting next week, [pause] unless I am mistaken,
[pause] and I hope I am, [pause] we will see an angry group
of shareholders possibly ripe for an approach, [pause] a
takeover bid that is, [pause] from some raider who wants to
profit from what I expect is only a temporary condition."

Appropriate pauses automatically slow our speech
to a manageable pace. They make it easier for the cross-
lingual audience to listen and to understand.

Pause in Place of Unnecessary Connectors and Stop-Gap Words

An unnecessary connector is any introductory
word, exclamation, or conjunction that is used repeti-

tively without contributing to the meaning or flow of the phrase. Commonly overused connectors are: *and, so, well, now, then, basically,* and *what I mean is.* These words cannot and should not be totally eliminated from speech, but we need to give some attention to whether they enhance the landscape of our thoughts or whether they are merely crabgrass in the lawn of our speech.

Stop-gap words are the guttural utterances that we use to fill space because we think it is the obligation of a speaker to be making noise all the time. Sensitive to the fact that all the eyes are on us, we use these sounds to buy the time to think. We would do better to buy our thinking time with a pause. Common stop-gap words are: *uh, um, er, and-uh, you know,* and *okay.*

Since those of us who frequently use unnecessary connectors and stop-gap words do so out of habit, we often do not know we are using them. When we audiotape ourselves, we can listen for and count these nonessential, disturbing utterances and take the first major step toward replacing them with pauses.

Pause After Headline, Sequencing, and Change of Topic Words or Phrases

Being a non-native English listener in a cross-lingual meeting is a bit like observing a thunderstorm. First you see the lightning and know the thunderclap is not far behind. The lapse between hearing a headline word that creates context, a sequencing word that maintains context, and a change of topic word that alters context is similar to the delay between the speed of light and the speed of sound. It is the momentary hesitation between hearing and understanding. The pause assures that the brief space between hearing and understanding is not

cluttered with other input before the message essential
for context has registered.

Example:
   "First, [pause] let's look at the February statistics. . . .
Now, [pause] let's see the first-quarter projections."

Pause Between Contrasting or Contradictory Ideas

Example:
   "On the one hand, the market is small, [pause] but on
the other hand, [pause] it is rich."

Example:
   "I don't like plan A, [pause] but plan B isn't much better."

Pause After Each Item on a List

It is difficult to mentally retain items on a list even
in the best of circumstances. A pause after each item
slows down our recitation of the list and allows the audience to register each item before we assail them with
subsequent ones.

Example:
   "We need to do several things to get the project started:
[pause] prepare the written copy; [pause] get departmental
approval; [pause] get estimates from printers; [pause] and
compile a mailing list."

Pause After Posing a Rhetorical Question

When we ask a rhetorical question, we do not demand an answer from the audience, do we? We ask

them only to consider the question, isn't that right? For this reason, rhetorical questions are wonderful techniques for involving the audience, aren't they? Rhetorical questions move the audience from a passive to an active state, but a rhetorical question will not be effective unless we pause long enough for the audience to mull it over and answer a private "yes" or "no."

Example:
"I'm sure many of you probably think we are going to settle out-of-court in the environmental damage suit, don't you? [long pause] Well, we're not!"

Pause for Emphasis

Less fluent non-native English speakers are able to conjure the overall gist of a conversation or the proceedings of a meeting while missing much of the detail. Those key details that are indispensable to the outcome we want to achieve can be highlighted by using the pause in combination with repetition.

Example:
"All business expense reimbursements must be made on form 1743. [pause] You will not be reimbursed unless you complete form 1743."

Enunciation/Pronunciation

How we pronounce words is a product of our environment and education. We acquire our mother tongue by listening to those around us when we are growing up and learning to speak. The major differences between British and American English are not grammatical, although a few minor differences do exist. The major differences are in some words (e.g., lift/elevator; flat/apartment; boot/trunk; bonnet/hood), in idioms and slang expressions, and in pronunciation. George Bernard Shaw once described Great Britain and the United States as "two countries divided by the same language."

In fact, there are more pronunciation variations within Great Britain itself than exist between England and the United States. In addition, there are scores of other countries that claim English as their national language, and each has its own particularities of pronunciation. We need not apologize for this. It is characteristic of languages, especially a language as diffuse as English. Every spoken language has national, regional, and often ethnic and class differences in both usage and pronunciation. We do not have to undo our own national, regional, ethnic, or class accent. First of all, it is quite difficult to do. Second, there is no reason to try.

For each person who declares that he or she can understand the British but not the Americans, there is someone else who swears that the British are impossible but the Americans are quite understandable. And let us not forget people who attended full-immersion English-language programs in Australia, Canada, Ireland, or some other English-speaking country and, as a result, have developed an ear for that country's way of speaking English. In my experience, whether a native English speaker is easy or hard to understand depends more on the habits and attitudes of the individual speaker than on the origin of the speaker. What we can do to assist comprehension is to speak whatever version of English is native to us with great care and lucidity. This suggests that many of us are sloppy in our speech and indeed we are. To become precise rather than sloppy, we can keep the following points in mind.

Relax the Jaw and Speak With the Mouth Open and the Lips Active

This advice may seem ridiculous. Doesn't everyone speak with an open mouth? No. At least not open enough to clearly articulate sounds. If we pay attention to other people when they speak, we will begin to notice how many people barely move their lips. The famous ventriloquist Edgar Bergen opened his mouth more widely when speaking for Charlie McCarthy than many of us do in normal conversation.

We should observe ourselves in a mirror or on videotape close up to discover how much we open our mouths and move our lips. If it is minimal, we should expand the mouth opening and the lip movement. We should also videotape ourselves to verify the result because the effort we make will feel more exaggerated to us than it will look and sound to the listener.

Do Not Swallow Vowels

Vowels between two consonants are frequently swallowed by native English speakers. For example, *fertile* can sound much like *futile* to a non-native English ear if the vowel between the *f* and the *r* is mangled either because we speak too quickly or do not move our lips enough. There are scores of other words. *Showed* can sound like *should* and *want* like *won't* to the non-native English speaker. The list is endless. Only context and good diction can reduce the opportunities for confusion.

Sometimes American business and professional men have poor articulation as a by-product of pushing the voice lower than its natural tone. There is a cultural stereotype that equates a low voice with masculinity and authority. The poor articulation occurs because in order to keep the voice in the chest, where the low tones resonate, the jaw needs to be tight, the mouth barely open, and the lips almost immobile. A famous American television news anchorman (who shall remain unnamed here) could be the poster boy for this phenomenon. Many of my clients with good English comprehension who follow the U.S. newscasts abroad have lamented their inability to understand this anchorman. Interestingly, my clients claim that they can understand American women newscasters better than American men newscasters, and I suspect it is due to this cultural stereotype of the manly voice and the bad habits necessary to produce it.

Articulate Consonants Especially in the Middle and at the End of Words

We commonly hit consonants extremely hard at the beginning of a word, slide over them in the middle of a word, and omit them completely at the end of a word. Lazy pronunciation of consonants results in so many words that sound alike to the cross-lingual audience that they cause confusion, such as *work* and *walk*, *weakness* and *witness*. A client told me that he and his colleagues sat through an entire press conference and thought the press secretary was saying *oracle* every time he said *article*. Not swallowing the *t* in *article* would have prevented this error.

Words such as *gonna* and *wanna* have become part of everyday English because we have played Pacman and eaten the vowel *i* and the consonant *g* in *going* and swallowed the letter *t* in *want*. The word *to* after both words has been completely devoured. Unfortunately, there are many other words or word combinations that suffer letter loss through imprecise pronunciation. A poorly articulated *can you* can quickly become the African country Kenya. A romp through *did you* becomes a mysterious object called a *dija*. These are words that have not become idiomatic and interfere with comprehension.

Special attention must be paid to word combinations where the last letter of the first word elides into the first letter of the second word, for example, *big gain, large earning*. These elisions are characteristic of English and contribute to its rhythm and cadence, but if not enunciated clearly, they can become one word *(bigane, largearning)*. A better solution is to talk about a *big earning* and a *large gain*.

Inflection

Stress, rhythm, and intonation are as important as pronunciation in conveying or contorting meaning. If we have any doubt, we need only read the following sentence aloud and shift the emphasis to the next word in the sentence each time we read it.

I didn't steal his pen.

Is this statement a matter of who is guilty?

I didn't steal his pen.

Or is it a robust denial?

I *didn't* steal his pen.

Maybe it is a matter of whether the pen was stolen or taken by mistake.

I didn't *steal* his pen.

Then again, perhaps it is not clear whose pen was stolen.

I didn't steal *his* pen.

Or perhaps it is not a pen that was stolen but a pencil.

I didn't steal his *pen*.

The answer is not where the guilt lies but where the stress lies.

Inflection also determines whether a statement is sincere or sarcastic. "Living on airplanes and in hotels is absolutely my favorite thing to do." Perhaps it is, perhaps it isn't—only the tone of voice will tell. We have all had the experience of being able to characterize a friend's mood by the way he or she says "Hello" when answering the phone.

Speakers characteristically speak in monotones or with a limited vocal variety for several reasons. First, we often have the misconception that being professional means repressing emotion. Second, our nervousness often is expressed through a physical freezing that restricts the voice, or conversely, in an attempt to control our nervousness, we overcontrol our vocal inflection. Finally, reading a speech or trying to recite it from memory can result in a monotonous delivery unless we are extraordinary readers or orators. Since inflection is essential to meaning, we should experiment to improve our vocal variety.

• *Speak with conviction.* Inflection is largely a matter of attitude. Simply saying things as though we meant them instead of unconsciously producing sound makes all the difference. Our emotion also keeps our listeners from becoming bored and will be a strong element in persuading them to follow our recommendations.

• *Pause and breathe.* Breath is fuel for the voice. Having adequate breath provides the energy to speak with conviction. Use the pause amply as already recommended.

• *Elongate vowels.* Elongating vowels means spending more time on them. One of the reasons that bel canto singing is so passionate is that singers learn to "ride the vowels." If we say the following phrases aloud, first in a matter-of-fact way, and then repeat them with conviction and an elongation of the capitalized vowel, we will hear a stark difference.

I think you look wOnderful!
This is the bEst quarter we have Ever had.
I lOve you.

Eye Communication

One of the strongest memories from my early days of trying to function in a foreign language is the tremendous fatigue I felt after an hour of highly concentrated listening. I remember that sometimes I would be tempted to tune out and give my ears and brain a rest.

What kept me tuned in was the eye contact of the person who was talking to me. Eye communication is quite natural in a one-on-one situation and, in fact, it comes across as rude or even suspect to evade looking at the person with whom we are having a conversation. It is much easier to avoid eye contact in a group situation. For this reason, it falls to the speaker to ensure that eye communication is not lost with a cross-lingual group. If the cross-lingual audience tunes out, even momentarily, they may lose the contextual thread necessary to stay on track with the speaker.

Eye communication with a group requires us to serially talk directly to individuals in the audience. Besides keeping them involved, eye communication will also aid understanding. Seeing the face and the lips of the speaker assists the ear in distinguishing the alien sounds of the foreign language.

We may find ourselves speaking in a culture where looking people in the eye is not common practice and may be offensive. We should not forget, however, that when we are in another culture, the people in that culture are generally expecting us to behave in accordance with who we are and where we come from. If we find ourselves in the curious position of trying to adapt our behavior to our cultural stereotypes of the audience while they are trying equally hard to adapt themselves to their cultural stereotypes of us, we will be like two ships passing in the night. Eye communication is a crucial nonverbal skill, so we should be well informed before we make the judgment call to abandon it.

We can appreciate the importance of the visual element as an aid to comprehension when we consider that in the human being, the optic nerve leading to the brain is twenty-five times larger than the auditory nerve leading from the ear to the brain. In speaking situations, visual stimuli far outweigh the auditory. Since the visual sense is so commanding, we need to enlist it as an ally rather than struggle with it as a competitor. The guiding rule for the effective use of eye communication is: *If our eyes are not looking at someone, our mouth should not be moving.* The specifics below elaborate how we can honor this guideline.

Talk From Notes Rather Than Reading

We can read four to five times faster than we can talk. It is a waste of the presenter's and the audience's time to read something that could just as easily be photocopied for the audience to read at the office, on the beach, in an airplane, or in the bathtub. There are few occasions in life where we read to people. The most common are reading stories to our children at bedtime and reading papers to audiences at conferences and meetings. When we read to our children, many times our objective is to put them to sleep. When we read to audiences at conferences and meetings, putting people to sleep is not our objective, but it is too often the result. If we read well, people will resist the urge to doze off, but we should not be surprised if many of our words are conquered by distractions either in the room or in the minds of our listeners.

When we read, we provide only auditory stimuli to the audience. The thirst for visual stimuli will be satisfied by daydreams or other objects in the room. Even if our subject commands attention, when we are engaged with the words on the paper and not with the audience, we make it much more taxing for the cross-lingual audience to stay focused on us.

I know that reading papers at academic and scientific conferences is such a strong tradition that few would want or dare to transgress it. In instances where we are committed to reading a paper, we should be so familiar with the content that we can glance at one or two sentences and know them well enough to be able to raise our eyes from the paper and look at the audience as we recite them. Papers read at academic conferences are usually going to be published, so whatever content the cross-lingual audience misses because of the absence of nonverbal aids can be compensated for by reading the published paper. Most speeches we give do not, however, fall into this category.

Divide the Audience Into Individuals

Complete several sentences or a thought with one individual before moving on to another. Be random, not regimented, in the eye pattern. Every audience is an aggregate of individuals. By focusing on individuals rather than the group, we establish a personal connection with each person. This sense of relationship compels the individual to pay attention and makes it easier for that person to concentrate and not drift.

Eye communication invites everyone's attention even when we are looking at only one person. The knowledge that we are serially shifting our attention from person to person makes the entire audience alert because they know that from time to time we will be looking at them.

Talking to individual audience members also helps us to speak at a natural pace with greater vocal inflection, as we are always more conversational when we talk to one person as opposed to an ocean of people. Most importantly, this technique allows us to use our eyes to monitor the attention and comprehension level of the listeners. If they look puzzled, it is a sign that we have lost them. If we cannot make eye contact with several people because they are looking out the window, contemplating the source of the carpet stains, or counting the stripes in the wallpaper, these are red flags that warn us to slow down and to repeat or paraphrase what we have said. Moreover, the cross-lingual audience is more disposed to ask questions for clarification and to respond to our question checks when they feel they have a relationship with us. Strong eye communication is the most powerful tool available to us for establishing this sense of relationship.

In Large Groups, Make Eye Contact With an Individual in Each Area of the Room

"Surely, you don't expect me to make separate eye contact with 200 people?" a stunned client asked. "I'm giving a ten-minute presentation on the new soft drink display for a chain of supermarkets, not reciting the whole of *War and Peace*." No, I am not suggesting that we turn our presentations into marathons, nor do I recommend running our eyes over the audience like a high-velocity scanner. When we are speaking in front of a large group, the distance between us and the audience permits us to make eye communication with selected individuals in different areas of the room and to create the illusion that we are looking at more people than we actually are. This phenomenon is sufficient to keep the entire audience engaged and in relationship with us, while providing us with feedback on how our message is being received. As in a smaller group, we should move randomly from one area to another. Each time we return to an area, we should look at a different person.

In a One-on-One Situation, Break Eye Contact Only Briefly

Eye contact should be interrupted only to think or to direct attention to samples, drawings, or written materials.

We do not want to assume a relentless stare when we talk with people one-on-one. In conversation, we customarily look at people when we talk to them, and they expect us to look at them when they speak to us. Occasionally we look away, but the looking away should be a purposeful act, not a nervous evasion. Looking away should be accompanied by a pause in speech or by an effort to focus the attention of the listener on something else. As a rule, one-on-one encounters with a non-native English speaker are easier to manage because the non-native English speaker is usually less intimidated about asking for clarification than in a group situation.

In a Small Group Around a Table, Serially Make Eye Contact With Everyone

In one sense, seated presentations are more comfortable for speakers because they are more informal than stand-up presentations, and we generally feel less vulnerable. The major error we make in seated presentations is that we are often seduced into directing our attention almost exclusively to one, two, or at most three people at the table. Usually, we speak to the people directly across from us or to the person we perceive as having the most authority. In a native-language situation, it is possible for the neglected members of the group to hear our comments, but they are left with the feeling of having overheard our presentation rather than having been included in it. The cross-lingual group shares the sensation of being left on the fringes if we do not look at them, but they will also be wanting in another way. If our stream of words is not directed to them, it risks becoming background noise, a sort of "verbal Muzak." Listeners may switch off and retreat into their own private thoughts.

It is a mistake to focus on a decision maker at the expense of other people in the meeting. We should always assume that everyone attending a meeting is there because they have an interest in what we have to say or will have input into any decisions that are made based on our intervention. Ignoring subordinates in a cross-lingual situation, besides being rude, is risky. Often the employees in the company with the best command of English are the secretaries. In some cases, they may be the only people at the meeting who understand the details and not just the gist. They will be consulted by the top directors after we have packed up our briefcase and headed for the airport. If we assume that they are at the meeting only to serve coffee and fetch pencils, we will be buried by our own hierarchical stereotypes.

In an Interview Situation, Look at the Interviewer and Not at the Audience or the Camera

In the event that we participate in an interview in front of an audience or are interviewed on television, we should be aware that this is different from a presentation to an audience. Even if we are seated in front of an audience in an auditorium or in front of "television land" in the case of a television interview, we are in conversation with the interviewer, not with the audience. Therefore, we should address our responses to the interviewer, not to the audience or to the television camera.

In both situations, the audience in the auditorium and in "television land" are observing our interchange with the interviewer. The same holds true when we are involved in conversation with panel members. Why does it make a difference where we look? At some level, the audience members know that they are eavesdropping on us. If we address them directly instead of staying engaged with the interviewer, we shift the dynamic and it looks as though we are snubbing the interviewer and making a plea to the audience. In a cross-lingual situation, it can even cause momentary confusion, leading the audience or viewers to think we are talking to them instead of responding to the interviewer.

Gestures

As a famous song from the Big Band era instructs, "Every little movement has a meaning all its own." Every language has gestures peculiar to it. The range of body language varies dramatically from language to language. In some languages, shaking the head from left to right means "yes" rather than "no." A twist like this can cause endless communication problems, but generally when a divergence between common English-speaking gestures and those of another country are so dramatic as to alter meaning, we are informed ahead of time or we learn very quickly. In my early days in Italy, I was addressing a group and made a gesture that I soon discovered was obscene to Italians. Did it damage my credibility? On the contrary—when I noticed the snickers and surprised expressions, I asked what I had done. After it was delicately explained to me, we all had a good laugh. If anything, this gaffe cemented my relationship with the group.

In addition to cultural differences in body language, individuals have their personal range of expression within the language. Some of us are reserved, others more expansive. The key is to use the range of expression that is natural for our personalities. Through years of teaching presentation skills and sitting through thousands of business and professional presentations, I can unequivocally say that most people shrink into "presentation mode" in front of a group and amputate much of their natural physical expression. For example, "Tie an Italian's hands behind his back and he can't speak," is a cliche that describes how physically expressive Italians are when they talk. I have been working with Italians for more than five years now, and have learned that even these masters of animated speech often leave their physical expression in their chairs when they stand up to speak in front of a group. If this habit of restricting our body language when we speak in front of a group is so diffuse, we must first ask ourselves why it is so widespread, and then answer the question, "Is it really all that important?"

When we stand up to address a group, all attention is riveted on us. It is as though one big eye were looking at us. This all-encompassing focus makes us feel vulnerable. One of the ways we seek to reduce our vulnerability is by making ourselves smaller and by putting barriers between ourselves and the audience. In the absence of a table or lectern to hide behind, all we have available to shrink and shield ourselves is our arms and hands, which we characteristically lock in some position and cease to use as we would in normal conversation. This is unfortunate because body language is a valuable tool for emphasizing and extending our message. Gestures and facial animation are essential for conveying meaning. As valid as gestures and facial animation are in any presentation, they assume an even greater value when speaking to the cross-lingual audience, who depend so strongly on visual messages to cross-check their verbal comprehension.

Use Facial Expression to Express Attitude and Emotions

The face is one of the major signs an audience reads to get a feeling about the presenter's attitude. What they see in our faces can determine whether they will be positively or negatively disposed toward us. Some of us naturally have an open, friendly face. And some of us tend to look like we are pushing a heavy boulder uphill even when our thoughts are lighthearted and sweat-free. For the most part, however, our faces reflect attitude and circumstance. Tension and nervousness result in a tight, overly severe expression or a frozen grin that suggests our undershorts are a size too small.

To find out what message the face is sending, close-up videotaping or the feedback of an honest friend who observes us giving a stand-up presentation are invaluable. Also, if we are emotionally in touch with ourselves, we can check in at any moment and ask ourselves, "What am I really feeling now?" The chances are good that our face will be reflecting that feeling. If we lean toward the "Listen or I'll break your fingers" look, we can soften the facial tone by reminding ourselves that in most instances the audience is kindly disposed to us and, in cross-lingual situations, they are often more tense than we are, as they are undergoing a language test as well as listening to our presentation.

Another attitude that contributes to an unwelcoming face is taking ourselves too seriously. The best way to counter this attitude is to paraphrase a famous T-shirt that says, "Life's too important to take seriously." Equally, our presentation is too important to take seriously.

Avoid Gestures That Are Distracting or Repetitive

Nonstop movement of the hands and nervous, repetitive gestures are disturbing to the audience. Since the cross-lingual audience needs to focus more intensely than the native English audience, we do not want to dilute their concentration on repetitive, meaningless movements. The most distracting gesture is locking the arms at the elbow and incessantly moving one arm up and down in a hammering, wood-chopping motion. This gesture adds nothing but annoying or hypnotic rhythm to our words. The best way to break this habit is to leave our hands relaxed at our sides when we are not gesturing. In this way, natural gestures will emerge, just as they do when we are speaking in a conversation.

Do Not Point at Someone in the Audience

A pointed finger smacks of the "Uncle Sam Needs You" poster and is generally unappreciated. A pointed finger puts people on the spot. Native English speakers may not like being on the long end of a pointed finger, but it is less intimidating for them than for the cross-lingual audience. The non-native English speaker who may understand the gist but not the detail of our comments might mistake the pointed finger as an invitation to respond in some way when, in fact, we are only using it as a gesture. Instead of the pointed finger, we should use the fully spread hand.

Use Gestures to Indicate Directions

The hardest words to master in a foreign language are the "little" words, for example, *up, down, over, under, in, out, through, around*. Non-native English speakers often confuse prepositions. Gestures are indispensable for helping the cross-lingual audience make distinctions.

Use Gestures to Illustrate or Emphasize Words

When we say our product launch was a gigantic or stupendous success, people who do not understand the words *gigantic* or *stupendous* will get the meaning if we open and extend our arms to signify *large*. When we rehearse our presentation, we should note words that we can make clearer through gestures.

Posture

How we stand and the way we hold our body suggests to others how we feel about ourselves. It also suggests to them how they should treat us, that is, what our *standing* will be with them. Since visual messages are so important in the cross-lingual environment, we need to devote some attention to the message we send with our posture.

Be Aware of the Impression Our Posture Creates

There are no rules about how we should come across. What is important is to know the impression we make and to decide whether that is the impression we want to give. We may want to come across as authoritative and reserved in some situations and more democratic and approachable in others. Whether we stand with our body rigid or relaxed sends a strong message to the audience about how accessible we are and how relaxed they can feel with us. A stiff posture intimidates. A casual posture can impress as arrogance. To determine the attitude we convey with our posture, we should videotape ourselves, rehearse in front of a mirror, or solicit the opinion of colleagues whose evaluations we trust.

Avoid Rocking or Swaying From Side to Side

Posture is a favorite place for our nervousness to manifest itself. If we plant ourselves with our weight leaning on one hip, we will invariably need to shift the weight at some point to the other hip. If we are nervous, we are prone to sway from hip to hip like a human metronome. A rocking, swaying movement draws audience attention away from what we are saying, so it becomes another comprehension hurdle for the cross-lingual audience. Balancing the weight on the balls of the feet and not locking our knees will defeat this distracting movement.

When Seated, Avoid Slouching or Rolling the Chair From Side to Side

Aimless motion distracts. Chairs with wheels beg to be in motion. We should resist their pleas.

Movement

Presentation skills seminars recommend moving with purpose as an audience involvement technique. Some go so far as to say we should never speak behind a lectern if we have a choice because the lectern is a barrier between the audience and the speaker. Since language is already a barrier with a cross-lingual audience, we could say that speaking behind a lectern in an international presentation puts a barrier in front of a barrier. In fact, large numbers of international presentations are delivered from lecterns. I do not believe that they are significant communication blocks if they are used correctly. Let us look at some techniques for using the lectern effectively, and then discuss how to incorporate movement if we are not speaking behind a lectern.

The Lectern Should Hold Our Notes, Not Us

A lectern is not a crutch. It exists to hold our notes. We should rest our hands lightly on the lectern, maintain an upright posture, and resist the temptation to lean on the lectern.

Maintain Eye Communication and Use Gestures

We have already noted the importance of eye communication and gestures for the cross-lingual audience. The major drawback of speaking behind a lectern is that we are seduced into reading, and we lose these nonverbal skills.

Adjust the Microphone

The microphone should not block the face or require us to bend down to speak into it. Anyone who watched the U.S. television news several years ago and observed Queen Elizabeth, "the talking wide-brim hat," can appreciate the importance of this advice. Unlike the typical elementary school class photo, the order of speakers at meetings and conferences is not determined by height. We need to adjust the situation to our needs rather than stretch or bend to adapt to it.

Move With Direction and Purpose by Letting Eye Communication Motivate the Movement

If we are not speaking behind a lectern, and we choose to walk around while we are speaking, we should avoid pacing back and forth like an expectant father. Aimless movement distracts, and more often than not, we end up talking to the walls, the ceiling, the floor, or our visual aids instead of to the cross-lingual audience. Movement should always have a reason, and the best reason is to approach someone we are talking to. Therefore, when we switch our eye communication from one audience member to another, we can take that opportunity to begin walking in the direction of the new person to whom we are talking. The formula is: look–talk–walk.

It is important to mention here that teaching presentation skills, as opposed to the teaching of debate or classic rhetoric, is a relatively new phenomenon that has developed in the United States since the late 1970s. It is only now beginning to spread to other countries. In many of the countries where we will be speaking, it is still common for people to write their speeches word for word and read them. Talking instead of reading; moving around instead of planting ourselves behind a lectern; looking people in the eyes and conversing with them instead of droning on with an occasional upward glance from our script are the exceptions rather than the rules. As a result, we may be afraid that we will be perceived as grandstanding if we deviate from the old mode. The overwhelming reason to take the risk by using the nonverbal techniques discussed above is that they work, and the cross-lingual audience will appreciate us for it.

5

Support Materials

Support materials are visual aids, handouts, or demonstration vehicles that help us to explain, to clarify, or to show how something works. Support materials are a valuable adjunct to a presentation because they are visual and sometimes directly involve the audience in doing something. Both of these features help to increase attention, comprehension, and retention of information.

Support materials play a special role with a cross-lingual audience because the ear does not have to bear the entire burden of understanding. Only those non-native English speakers who have lived in an English-speaking country for an extensive period of time or those who had an English-speaking caretaker during their early years of childhood have acquired English primarily *by ear*. Most non-native speakers have *learned* rather than *acquired* the language. Their *passive* vocabulary is much larger than their *active* vocabulary. As a result, their reading comprehension is superior to their listening comprehension. They recognize more words visually than they do aurally, and they do not have to struggle with problems consequent to rapid speech, unclear pronunciation, or strange, unfamiliar accents. For these reasons, the visual supports are especially important, provided they remain faithful to their denotative function and *support* rather than substitute or overwhelm the presentation. We should be attentive to:

1. Selecting the most effective support material
2. Appropriately choosing the specific content and design of our support material
3. Using the support material in a way that adds to the message of our presentation rather than detracts from it

Entire books have been written on the proper development and use of support materials. We discuss only those elements that are most relevant to cross-lingual situations.

Handouts

A handout is printed material related to our presentation that we give to the audience. Common handouts are copies of our visual aids (usually when they are in the form of overhead transparencies), budget printouts or accounting spreadsheets, written proposals, and even a copy of the speech itself. The effectiveness of a handout depends on (1) what it is, (2) when we distribute it, and (3) how we make reference to it.

Distribute a One-Page Outline or Summary of the Presentation at the Beginning of the Presentation

A one-page outline of our presentation is an indispensable aid to the cross-lingual audience. It clearly establishes context, sequence, and change of direction. As it is an outline, it should be skeletal and should bullet the main points and subpoints with no more than one to three words per heading.

Providing an outline is analogous to giving a stranger a tourist map of London as opposed to one of the copiously detailed *A-ZED* books, which list every street and lane. Just as a tourist generally wants a guide to the key places of interest, so the cross-lingual audience requires a major sense of direction and a mention of the high points to be visited during the course of our comments. Listeners do not require our more complex, detailed notes because we are in the driver's seat, not the audience.

Handouts Distributed Prior to or During the Presentation Should Be Short

These handouts should not contain more information than the cross-lingual audience can easily read within thirty seconds to one minute. Written material begs to be read. Human curiosity dictates that as soon as we distribute written material to the audience, they immediately set about examining it to see what it is. If it is interesting, they will become absorbed in it. By providing an audience with too much written material, we create our own distraction. The audience does not know whether to pay attention to what we are saying or to what we have handed them. This point takes on added importance with the cross-lingual audience who invariably opts for the handout due to their greater proficiency with the written word.

To avoid splitting audience attention, we should direct them to the material we have given them, ask them to review it, and wait silently while they read it. Cross-lingual audiences may need more time to read our material than a native-language audience. In a native-language situation, a speaker is advised to ask the audience to put the outline away so that reference to it will not take attention away from the speaker. The cross-lingual audience, on the other hand, may need to make occasional reference to the outline. It gives them a greater sense of security and can help them stay on track with us or to get back on track with us should they lose the context. The primary caution is that we must confine the handout to key points.

Distribute Lengthy, Detailed Handouts After the Presentation

Give people a sea of information, and they will go swimming in it. They may even drown. It takes time to read and to analyze lengthy, detailed information. The lengthy handout challenges our audience to do this while we are speaking at the expense of listening to the speech. If we write more clearly than we speak, and our discourse only replicates what we have given our audience in writing, we should consider that the presentation is probably a waste of their time and of ours. It might be wiser to communicate in writing before the meeting or conference, ask members of the prospective cross-lingual audience to study the material, and advise them that the subsequent meeting will be a discussion of what they have read.

One exception when we might do well to provide a detailed handout during the course of a presentation rather than afterward is when we are in a working meeting and the group needs to pore over an extensive list of numbers or specifications. Even in this instance, we should parcel out the material page by page, making available only that information central to the issue being discussed at a particular point in the meeting. To do otherwise is to risk provoking questions and discussion out of sequence. When we have a cross-lingual audience, we must avoid this departure from structure because all semblance of context and sequence will be lost, seriously affecting audience comprehension and their ability to respond in a working meeting.

Copies of Slides or Overhead Transparencies Should Be Distributed After the Presentation

If the audience has been given our visual aids in handout form at the outset of our presentation, there is little reason for them to look at the visual aids during the presentation. As with the untimely distribution of lengthy handouts, we split the audience's attention. Should they look at the visual aid in their hands or the one on the screen at the front of the room? The advantage of drawing the audience's attention to the visual aids on display is that we can control where the audience looks, when they look, and for how long. We can also surmise from their facial expressions whether the visual aid is clear or whether it requires more explanation.

If we are going to distribute copies of the visual aids to the audience at the end of the presentation, we should tell them that we intend to do so at the beginning of the presentation. This will reduce their anxiety about having to remember everything and will keep them from losing the thread of what we are saying because they are copying the visual aids as notes.

Demonstrations

Demonstrations are most effective for selling an object or piece of equipment; for showing how something works; or to teach people how to perform a particular task. Demonstrations are especially effective with cross-lingual audiences because they appeal to the senses and utilize motor activities. Words take a back seat to action. Demonstrations can be used for purposes as diverse as training someone to use a highly sophisticated computer system to the seemingly simple task of filling in a form. They are powerful because they involve the audience. The Chinese philosopher Confucius is supposed to have said: "I hear and I forget. I see and I remember. I do and I understand."

Arrange the Demonstration so That Everyone Is Involved

If we are showing a group how to use a computer system, we should arrange for everyone to have a terminal. If it is not possible to have a terminal for each person, we should make certain that everyone has the opportunity to practice all the functions we are teaching by demonstration.

Allow Time to Monitor the Work of the Group

Filling in forms, for example, is an especially hard task to perform in a foreign language. The style of forms and the language and symbols for marking responses can differ dramatically from language to language and even from country to country within the same language. Therefore, if we are showing the group how to fill in a new order form that has been drawn up for the company, we should have a visual aid to demonstrate it and blank forms for the group to complete. We should allow ourselves time to move around the room and make certain that everyone has understood. If the group is too large for individual monitoring, we may need assistants for this purpose. If assistants are not available, we can monitor by asking questions.

Visual Aids

Visual aids can be an invaluable tool for communicating to cross-lingual audiences. They are so crucial to establishing and maintaining context and augmenting comprehension and recall that we should never make a presentation without them. Still, we should not fall on the other side of the horse and have so many visual aids that the audience feels as if they are viewing a subtitled motion picture without the motion. The art in using this powerful cross-lingual communicative medium is to know (1) which type of visual aid to use (flip chart, overhead transparency, slides, or video); (2) what information needs to be visually represented and how to represent it; and (3) how to use visual aids.

Selecting the Right Type of Visual Aid

Just as we often decide what to wear on a given day based on criteria such as what is ironed, we often select our visual aids according to what is at hand or otherwise convenient for us. Instead, we should take into consideration the formality of the presentation, the size of the group, the purpose and content of the presentation, and the amount of interaction we want to have with the audience.

Flip Charts

Flip charts are most effective with small groups (twenty-five or less), in informal meetings, and in highly interactive presentations, brainstorming sessions, or working meetings. For flip charts to work, the group has to be small enough that everyone in the room can see the flip chart. The writing on the flip chart must be large and legible. This information seems obvious until we conduct a mental inventory of all the presentations we have sat through where the effort to decipher the writing on the flip charts surpassed the energy devoted to resolving the problem under discussion.

Because flip charts allow us to record information in the moment, it is always a good idea to have one accessible when we speak to a cross-lingual group. If we are alert and sensitive to our audience, the presence of the flip chart will permit us to write down key words when a scan of questioning faces suggests we know something our audience doesn't know and will probably never find out if we don't make it visual.

If we are speaking to a cross-lingual group who all share one language, it is helpful to have two flip charts. During brainstorming sessions, suggestions from the group can be recorded in English on one flip chart while a fluent English-speaking member of the cross-lingual audience can record the information in the group-shared native language on the other.

Slides

Slides are best used in formal presentations to large groups in excess of 150 people. Speakers sometimes prefer to use slides for all the reasons that generally make this form of visual aid a bad choice for cross-lingual presentations if it is not used with care. Slides provide a great way for us to "be there without being there"; all we have to do is turn off the lights and click from slide to slide while we read the accompanying script, frequently in a disembodied monotone. The problem, of course, is that while we are in hiding, we lose connection with the audience. We can't see them and they can't see us. It is impossible for us to monitor whether our message is being received or not, and we rob the cross-lingual audience of the crucial visual cues they require to better understand us.

If we use slides, we should use them sparingly. The lights should not be turned off for more than ten minutes (or until we hear someone snore) without turning them on again and making contact with the audience by either asking questions or speaking to them directly without slides. Once the contact has been made, we can return to another short segment of the slide show.

Overhead Tranparencies

Overhead transparencies are the most versatile visual aid for use with cross-lingual audiences. Overhead transparencies can be used with audiences of all sizes. Since overhead transparencies allow us to keep the room lights on, we are liberated to interact with the cross-lingual audience. We can maintain eye contact and are free to gesture and move, all of which help the cross-lingual audience to stay attentive and to understand us. It is now possible to generate highly professional images through computer graphics, so it is advisable for us to use the overhead projector where slides used to dominate.

Presenting a Video

Do not allow a videotape to stand alone as the presentation. It is tempting to let technology do our work for us. A well-produced video can succeed in gaining and maintaining the interest of the cross-lingual audience, but it does little to enable us to establish a relationship with them. A video should be introduced by us and positioned so that the audience is prepared for what they will be watching. A preview of what they will see should also be given. The length of a video should not run more than fifteen or twenty minutes.

After the showing of the videotape, we should summarize what the audience has seen, emphasizing the essential points we want them to remember. Unlike other visual aids, a video is more global and less selective in its images. It tells more of the story, whereas an overhead transparency captures only the chapter headings or the main events. We need to be sure that what people remember is what we would like them to remember. At the close or the summary, we should entertain questions from the group.

Choosing the Content of Visual Aids

Although we may have been taught that there is a dichotomy between objectivity and subjectivity, and that objectivity is more highly valued in making business and professional decisions, in fact, audiences are not objective. They do not accept or reject ideas in isolation from their feelings about the person who presents or represents those ideas. How the audience feels about us will greatly influence their receptiveness to what we have to say. As a result, visual aids can never be a stand-in for us, but only an adjunct.

The purpose of visual aids for any audience is to increase attention, comprehension, and retention. For the cross-lingual audience, they must also create context and establish sequence.

Be Visual

As the adage informs, "A picture is worth a thousand words." It can take a non-native speaker of English a considerable amount of time to add a thousand words to his or her English vocabulary. It is much more useful to provide a picture that leaps over all language barriers. An additional reason to use pictures, graphs, diagrams, and symbols is that recent brain research indicates that many memory cues are stored in the right hemisphere of the brain. The right hemisphere attends more to visual tasks while the left hemisphere attends to the verbal. This cohabitation of visual cues and memory in the same hemisphere of the brain explains what happens when we encounter someone we met long ago and are able to recall that person's face, but not his or her name. Graphic visual aids will help our cross-lingual audience hold onto a concept even if their vocabulary doesn't permit them to name it.

Simplify! Simplify! Simplify!

A good visual aid is like an effective billboard or road sign. It captures attention and gives the essential information for orientation and recall in a split second without dangerously diverting the driver's attention from the business of driving. A good visual aid should contain the minimum of information to focus attention on the main point(s). Complete sentences are an encumbrance. Too many words will concentrate the cross-lingual audience on grammatical structure and sentence word order when all that they need is one word or symbol to maintain context and guide sequence.

> *Example: Benefits*
> 1. Profit
> 2. Maintenance
> 3. Resale

If the Audience Shares a Language, Caption Visual Aids in Both English and the Shared Language

Our presentation isn't an English proficiency exam, so our audiences, no matter how good their English, will appreciate our efforts to reduce their efforts. When captioning visual aids in the shared language of our cross-lingual audience, it is advisable to have the visual aids prepared or checked by someone fluent in the language. Translation from one language to another often is not literal. First, there are false friends—words that look and sound alike but have different meanings. For example, *factory* in English is often confused by Italians with *fattoria* meaning "farm." In addition, words that seem to mean the same in English and the foreign language may not be used in the same context by a native speaker of the language. An example is the word *presentation* as in *business presentation*. Though Latin languages have a version of this word that is quite similar, the word is more commonly used in the context of introductions. Another word is more frequently invoked to describe a speech given for business or professional purposes.

A native speaker of the language can help us where a dictionary might lead us astray. And what if no one is available to provide this service for us? It still won't hurt for us to give it a try on our own. Even if we make a mistake, the gesture of trying to help our cross-lingual audience will, more often than not, result in our mistake being taken in good cheer. It may even serve as a basis for cementing our relationship with the audience, as our listeners are always less intimidated about making mistakes in our language if we also make mistakes in theirs. It puts us in the same boat, and nothing brings people together quite as effectively as the opportunity to laugh together over our shared humanity. *A word of caution:* We should never deliberately try to make a mistake for the purpose of bringing about camaraderie. Manipulation and lack of authenticity carry an odor, and our audience will most surely sniff us out.

Represent Numbers on Graphs, Pie Charts, or Bar Graphs

English numbers can be especially problematic. The pronunciation differences between *thirteen* and *thirty,* *fifteen* and *fifty,* or *nineteen* and *ninety,* for example, are quite small, but the numerical differences are quite large if we're talking about an outlay of \$19,000 versus \$90,000. Therefore, it is valuable to always represent numbers in writing, and when comparing numbers to represent them on graphs and charts.

People remember trends and relationships more

readily than specific numbers. Charts and graphs show major trends and relationships and are also helpful to the cross-lingual audience because the many words English speakers use to indicate trends—for example, *go up, go down, rise, decline, fall off, drop off, peak, crash*—may not be quickly grasped by the listener, and the adjectives that surround these words—such as *sharp, steady, dramatic*—may get lost altogether. A pictorial representation leaves little room for confusion. Charts and graphs should focus on overall trends only. Computer printouts with columns of numbers should be given as handouts at the close of a presentation or distributed piecemeal during a working session. They are not visual aids!

Convert Financial Figures Into Local Currency

Represent the dollar equivalent along with the local currency on the visual aid, and represent each currency in a different color if using multicolored visual aids. Most people's daily work does not involve converting currency rates. Giving financial data in dollars in a cross-lingual situation without giving the corresponding local currency can confuse a lot of people. They want to know the cost in terms of what is in their wallets, not ours. If the information is not readily provided for them, they may take a short mental vacation out of frustration or immediately set about trying to work out the conversion. While they are mentally away, they will miss important subsequent information.

Print All Written Data in Large Capital Letters

Visual aids are not handouts. They must be seen and absorbed from a distance. Slides should be professionally prepared and overhead transparencies computer-generated when possible. Lettering should be at least 10-point double width, ideally larger. If the information does not fit using this print size, it is a red flag that we are probably making our visual aids too wordy.

Handwritten visual aids should be printed in large uppercase letters. Even languages with the same alphabets as English may vary in the way some of the lowercase letters are written. Common differences occur in the handwritten versions of the vowels *a*, *e*, and *o*, and in some consonants such as *f*, *m*, and *n*. Numbers and letters that are generated by hand should be printed as they appear on standard keyboards for typewriters or word processors.

Using Visual Aids

The most effectively composed visual aids will quickly be rendered ineffective if we display and use them ineptly. A few tips can help us avoid the possible pitfalls.

Placement

When possible, place the flip chart stand or the screen at an angle at one side of the front of the room. We do not always have to settle for the room as we find it. Meeting rooms are set up in particular ways out of habit. Habitual practices are not necessarily the ones that work best. There is a story in psychoanalytic folklore that the time-honored tradition of the analyst placing herself or himself behind the couch was the result of Freud's timidity and embarrassment about the sexual revelations of his patients. Allegedly, he was more comfortable not having to look them in the eye. As a result, a ponderous theoretical rationale was developed and perpetuated to justify the practice. The Freud story may or may not be true, but the possibility that the person who designed the first meeting room was someone who never had to give a presentation before a group is highly probable; that it was someone who didn't know much about what goes into making a good presentation is a certainty.

Habits are quite resilient. The common tradition of centering screens on the front wall of the room, of placing overhead projectors at one end of a conference table, inevitably in the middle, or of placing flip chart stands in the center of the room persists in spite of the fact that as speakers we have to be contortionists to avoid blocking our own visual aids. Too many of us also fail to notice that the lumbering size of some overhead projectors blocks the view of some of the people seated around a conference table. The problem is relevant with any audience. It assumes greater dimensions with the cross-lingual audience due to the primary importance of visual aids as tools for comprehension.

Timing

Reveal a visual aid only when it is time to talk about it and remove it when it is no longer relevant. Let us never forget that visual aids create, maintain, and shift context for the cross-lingual audience. If we reveal a visual aid before we are ready to talk about it, at best we will distract the audience, and at worst we will confuse them. Because visual stimuli overwhelm nonvisual stimuli, the audience will inevitably look at the visual aid. The native English audience will simply be distracted by it. They will look at it and wonder when we will get around to talking about it. The cross-lingual audience is more likely to try to match it with what we are saying. If we have not verbally caught up to the visual aid, our cross-lingual audience might just opt to focus on the visual aid and not listen to us at all. Similarly, if we keep a visual aid in front of the listeners after we have moved on to another point, it will continue to command their attention. The cross-lingual audience will miss an important shift in our presentation because we failed to signal it.

Mechanics

Do not talk while changing flip chart paper, slides, or overhead transparencies. Pause while turning, advancing, or positioning the visual aid, then begin to talk about it. Fiddling with visual aids is disturbing to the eyes and irritating to the ears of the audience. Background noises that may be incidental to a native speaker who is able to accurately fill in any words lost to the competing sound are a major source of interference to the non-native English speaker.

Timing

Before commenting on a visual aid, give the audience time to look at it and take it in. The audience needs an opportunity to position the visual aid in their mind's eye for a few seconds before having to return their attention to the presenter. Whatever remarks we make in relation to the visual aid will then be grasped and retained more readily. This is especially valid for the cross-lingual audience when the visual aids display numbers or words instead of pictures or symbols.

Talking

Do not have a conversation with the visual aid. Visual aids seduce not only the audience but often the speaker. It is tempting to position ourselves in such a way that we begin to talk to our visual aids instead of to the audience, preventing the non-native English speakers from seeing our face when we speak. If we concentrate our attention on the visual aid and continue to look at it and refer back to it long after it has served its purpose, we risk sending the message to the cross-lingual audience that we are still discussing the same point when, in fact, we may have shifted to another. Just as readily, our absorption in the visual aid may suggest that we have returned to an earlier point when we have not.

Do not talk while writing on a flip chart or overhead transparency. The cross-lingual audience needs to see our face while we are talking. If we are writing on a flip chart or an overhead transparency, our back will be turned to the audience or we will be looking down. The voice usually becomes less audible, and the audience is unable to see our eyes and lips, removing two major sources of communicative cues. We should write first and then talk. It is a good Hitchcockian technique that creates suspense. The audience wonders what we are writing, so they become more involved. It also gives the cross-lingual audience a chance to copy what we have written without having to split their attention between what we are writing and what we are saying.

6

Audience Participation

Audience participation refers to interaction between the speaker and audience during the course of the presentation itself. It should be distinguished from question and answer sessions that customarily follow a presentation. The primary rationale for audience participation is that it involves the audience, and involvement increases retention. People remember things they have actively participated in more readily than they recall information passively received. Involving the cross-lingual audience serves the added purpose of giving the non-native English speakers an opportunity to clarify concepts or language that mystify them. It also provides us with important feedback on the audience's comprehension level. If the audience does not respond to the questions we pose in a way that suggests they have understood us, chances are quite high that they have not.

As speakers, we are in charge of soliciting and managing audience participation. We should not give the audience unlimited freedom to interrupt with questions or comments because we could lose control of the presentation. If the linear quality of our thinking is lost, the context needed by the cross-lingual audience for understanding will go out the window as well.

The most common ways to request audience participation are demonstrations and questions. Demonstrations are often the best means of teaching someone to
do something. For example, we learn how to drive a car
by getting in the car, shifting gears, choking out a few
times, and making a bevy of mistakes before we get to
the end of the street. We make these errors in execution
even if we have spent hours glued to a manual telling
us exactly what to do because learning from the written
or spoken word is only analytical. The part of our brain
that controls motor skills has not yet had adequate access to the task. (Suggestions on using demonstrations
as an interactive technique are included in Chapter 5.)

Many presentations, however, are a matter of conveying information and persuading the audience to take
action based on that information. In these instances, the
best way to involve the audience is through the use of
questions. The major categories of questions are:

- Rhetorical questions that do not require an audible response. For example, "There is a lot of talk
  in the company that our own independent research program will suffer if we accept the gov-
  ernment contract, isn't there?"
- Questions asking for some form of audience response such as a show of hands or a voice vote.
  For example, "How many of you have had a
  chance to read the proposal from the Marketing
  Department? Would you raise your hands
  please?"
- A solicited example, such as, "I understand there
  have been a lot of problems with the new computer system. Could someone give me an example of how it has interfered with your work?"

Asking the cross-lingual audience to participate must be done with delicacy. We may put people on the spot and embarrass them. Mother-tongue English speakers or the most fluent non-native English speakers could dominate speakers who are less fluent or less confident of their English-language skills.

Facilitating Participation

Use Only Rhetorical Questions if a Close or Continuing Relationship With the Audience Has Not Yet Been Established

If we have worked with the audience previously or have been able to rapidly develop an informal relationship with them, we have a certain sensitivity about the degree of involvement we can demand from them. In the absence of this familiarity with the audience, rhetorical questions are preferable. This type of question involves the audience without subjecting individuals to what may feel like a high-pressure test of their language skills. All a rhetorical question requires is a shake of the head, a quiet "yes" or "no" that mixes with the responses of other audience members, or a silent pondering of the question that takes place in the privacy of one's own head.

When a speaker poses a question, it can make people feel as though they are back in school. This is not a sentimental journey for everyone unless they were hotshots then and continue to be now. This situation is valid for all speaking environments, but is especially charged for the cross-lingual audience. People able to answer our question quite brilliantly in their own language may be unable to respond quickly with breadth and depth in English. As a result, they may feel that others will get the impression that they are stupid or superficial when, in fact, they are quite intelligent and knowledgeable. This fear of projecting a negative, false impression can encourage them to remain silent. If, however, we are talking to a homogeneous group of people who work together frequently and already know each other's capabilities, the problem of "losing face" based on a false impression is diminished. Similarly, if we have developed a close, ongoing relationship with a group, its members will feel less vulnerable to our judgment of them than they will with someone who is an unknown entity.

A Question Requiring a Show of Hands or Voice Vote Should Be Preceded by an Introductory Statement and a Pause

Listening to a person in a foreign language can be like a long-distance international telephone call with a slight delay on the line. If we require audience response, we can increase our odds of getting it by signaling the cross-lingual audience to listen more closely because we intend to ask them a question.

Example:
"I would like to ask a question. [pause] How many of you think we should reduce the number of administrative offices?"

Put the Question in Its Simplest Form

If the question is too complicated, the audience may forget what we asked by the time we get to the end of it.

With questions, as with statements, we should always keep it simple without being simplistic.

Example:
"If you are interested in learning more about flextime, please raise your hand."

[versus]

Example:
"Based on what you've heard about the system of flextime that is being discussed by top management, how many of you would be willing to explore the various ways that it can be implemented in your particular department?"

Demonstrate to the Audience the Form Their Response Should Take

If we want people to raise their hands, we should raise our hand as a gesture to show them how they should give their response. Cultures have different ways of indicating assent and dissent. We need to specify the form that we recognize.

Example:
"If you agree to change the conference from April to July, please raise your hand." [raising our hand as we say it]

Example:
"If you support the strike, say 'yes.' Do you support the strike?"

If Examples Are Solicited, Give the Group Time to Formulate and Think About How to Express Them in English

Many non-native English speakers who do not have words and phrases at the tip of their tongues are able to express themselves with confidence, depth, and clarity if we give them time to formulate their comments. When we want raw material from the group, we must provide a minute or two of quiet time to allow them to pull their thoughts together in English and to rehearse these thoughts in their own minds before addressing the group. We must also recognize that there will be people who speak English extraordinarily well, are proud of their fluency, and may want to use our presence as an opportunity to exercise their fluency. We should be careful to not lean too heavily on these people when we ask questions. We can risk falling into a dialogue with one person at the expense of group involvement.

Example:
"I'm interested in how this division has been maintaining low production costs. Take one or two minutes to think about your department; then I'd like each of you to tell me what you are doing to keep production costs low."

It may also be helpful to write the question on a visual aid to focus group thinking.

Give Everyone an Opportunity to Speak

Too often international presentations are like television quiz shows where the person who can push the buzzer first gets to answer the question. A major complaint of non-native English speakers is that native English speakers monopolize the interactive part of presentations. Native English speakers are more likely to have a nonstop connection between their thoughts and their tongues, whereas non-native English speakers often feel as though they are on an elevator traveling to the top floor of the World Trade Center and someone has pushed all the floor buttons.

In a small group, we can go around the table and ask each person if he or she would like to comment. We should make it clear that people may decline this offer. In addition, we should follow an established order when we go around the table or room so that people know when their turn will come. Randomness can create anxiety.

If Appropriate, Send a Memo Regarding Group Discussion

When the presentation is part of a meeting and we want group discussion, we should send a memo in advance to all participants and list the areas demanding individual or group discussion. Talking on a subject with little or no preparation time is difficult for many people even when language does not loom as an issue. Most of us would prefer to know in advance the subject to be discussed. In general, it makes for more productive meetings. In a cross-lingual situation, it can mean the difference between a one-person show and a lively, creative encounter among colleagues.

Languages are taught as communicative functions. People learn best and fastest those words and phrases they need in order to survive and thrive in particular situations. Giving a cross-lingual audience advance notice of the areas where their thinking will be requested or required allows them to target the vocabulary and language functions they will need to review in order to participate with confidence and competence in the meeting.

7

Question-and-Answer Sessions

The question-and-answer session is not to be confused with the asking of questions during the course of the presentation (see Chapter 6). We put questions to the audience during the presentation to hold their attention and to increase their retention. In any case, when we use questions as an audience participation technique, we are the author of the questions in both form and content. The question-and-answer session is different. The audience becomes the inquisitors with another set of objectives. They may want us to clarify what we have said, to explain it in greater depth, or to expand upon it. They may also want to challenge our data, our conclusions, or even our personal or professional integrity. From the presenter standpoint, the question-and-answer period allows us to clarify our discourse, to expand the range and depth of our argument, and to add anything we may have forgotten to mention during the presentation. It also gives us a shot at rebutting any opposing views that may linger at the end of the presentation or that are raised during the question-and-answer session.

Sometimes we have to remind ourselves of the benefits of entertaining questions from the audience because conducting a question-and-answer session is a bit like hang gliding. Though we have a measure of control over our direction, there is always the possibility that a strong wind may unexpectedly blow us off course and threaten to entangle us in high tension wires. People who are opposed to our ideas can become hostile and attack us. Others may use the question-and-answer period to test our reaction to adversity. We are more vulnerable when we open the floor to questions. This vulnerability can deteriorate into a conspicuous self-consciousness as our confidence drops below our ankles like a pair of old socks. As a result, we often approach question-and-answer sessions with apprehension. In fact, we should welcome them.

The conversational quality of a good question-and-answer session is by far a more natural form of communication than the often stilted, authoritative one-way street of the presentation itself. The uniqueness of the question-and-answer environment with the cross-lingual audience is that it is a vulnerable period for them as well—often more vulnerable than it is for the presenter. Unless there has been a high level of interaction during our presentation, the audience has been passive recipients of our discourse. How much they have heard and understood of our remarks is a personal matter for each audience member until the question-and-answer period when our invitation to participate is both a comprehension test and an exposure of their ability to speak English.

Perhaps more than any other part of our presentation, the question-and-answer session is highly dependent on our attitude and intentions. We need to be totally present with all of our senses and sensitivity. We must look and listen rather than just talk. We must harness patience, flexibility, spontaneity, and more than a small dose of humor and goodwill.

The following guidelines will promote a productive question-and-answer session. These guidelines may blatantly contradict the suggested techniques for use with an audience of native English speakers.

Question-and-Answer Guidelines

Use Body Language in Addition to Words to Encourage Questions

Our physical behavior strongly communicates how we feel about receiving questions from the audience. Children at the inchoate stage of language acquisition read the moods of a parent from the subtleties of posture, gestures, facial expression, and tone of voice. Similarly, the cross-lingual audience can sense how we are likely to treat them and their questions by tuning into and interpreting the nonverbal messages we send them.

It isn't enough to say, "I'd be glad to answer any questions." Our voice must sound pleased and our body language must be inviting. We should move closer to the audience rather than back away from them; relax our face and smile rather than knit our brow or look as though we were modeling for Mt. Rushmore; spread our arms in an open, embracing gesture rather than fold them across the chest, lock them behind our back, or clasp them nervously in front of us; and, finally, we should raise our hand to indicate what we want them to do to signal their readiness to ask a question.

Prepare a Sample Question

A presentation or a speaker can be so provocative or inspiring that audience members will be jockeying for the chance to ask a question. We have excited them and bully for us for having created such robust interest. Unfortunately, business and professional presentations are more often than not followed by less enthusiastic responses. People may have been interested in what we had to say, but not inspired. A biological monograph on the mating habits of flatworms or the new policy for inputting distribution codes for merchandise can be presented in a way to stir enthusiasm and admiration, but they seldom are. Still, the audience is there because they have either an interest in our subject or a need for the ideas and information we will convey.

Sometimes dead air at the beginning of a question-and-answer session indicates that we have dispatched the details so tidily that no more need be said, but we should not dash too quickly to the bar or the door until we are certain that this is the case. The audience might need a jumpstart before they smoothly cruise into asking questions. Frequently, many people in the audience have a question but each person wants to ask the second question; few people want to ask the first. To some extent, each person is waiting to see how the presenter will respond to questions. The audience knows that the dynamic of interaction has changed for us as well as them. We have probably all had an experience where the speaker seems to become another personality during the question-and-answer session. If a penetrating, challenging question transforms Gandhi into Attila the Hun, chances are the enthusiasm for asking questions will be quickly dampened. Another factor contributing to the lull between the request for questions and the asking of one is that people may think that their question is inappropriate in some way or not what the presenter wants. Once one or two people who do not have this concern ask a question, the more reticent audience members often summon their courage to participate.

Cross-lingual audiences may require more time to phrase the question in English. By supplying a sample question, we let the audience know that we sincerely want questions; we give them time to think of a question; we set some standard for the type of questions we expect; we give them time to phrase the question in English; and we demonstrate that the respect and cordiality that (hopefully) characterized our presentation will be extended to the question-and-answer session.

Example:
"I'd be pleased to answer any questions. Does anyone have a question?" [raising our hand to encourage] [dead air for several seconds] A question I'm often asked is 'How much time is needed to train workers on the new system?' "

Repeat the Question Before Answering It

With an audience of native English speakers, we do not need to repeat a question unless it was not heard by everyone. In fact, to repeat a question that was heard and understood might appear to be condescending or a thinly veiled attempt by the speaker to buy time while searching for ways to tap dance around the issue. The cross-lingual audience has different needs. It often is not enough to hear something only once to understand it sufficiently. Many non-native English speakers get the gist of a question the first time they hear it and fill in important details the second time. Also, we must remind ourselves that in a cross-lingual audience, questions will be asked with a wide range of accents. Even people who speak the same native language (i.e., all French, all German, all Spanish) will speak English with differing accents depending on when they learned English, their method of study, the accent of their teacher, and the non-native speaker's aural and pronunciation skills.

In addition, someone who is accustomed to hearing English with a French accent may never have heard English with a Hungarian accent. The audience has listened to us give the presentation, so they have had ample time to tune their ears to our voice and accent. Consequently, if we repeat the question, more people are likely to understand it. Of course, if we are less comprehensible than the person who posed the question, the audience probably missed the bulk of our presentation anyway, and will be equally unable to follow our answer to the question. If, however, we have been sensitive to the suggestions and guidelines outlined in these chapters, we should be able to reinforce the clarity of a questioner who speaks English well or to provide clarity for an interrogator who does not.

If the Question Needs Paraphrasing, Confirm With the Questioner That the Paraphrasing Is Accurate

The question may be asked in a long, complicated way that needs to be simplified before it is repeated. It may also be asked in fractured English and may be difficult for everyone to understand, including the presenter.

Example:

[Question]

"Is true money we will lost if we do together three divisions not two?"

[Paraphrase]

"You want to know if we will lose money if we have three divisions instead of two, is that right?"

In Some Situations, Writing Down Questions Is Best

In groups of seventy-five people or more, distribute blank 3-by-5-inch cards before the presentation to permit the audience to write their questions after the presentation. Many people are intimidated by speaking in front of large groups. Any discomfort with language proficiency will exacerbate this intimidation while creating it in those who are normally not hesitant to speak in front of large groups in their own language. Though some non-native English speakers can speak English better than they can write it, as we have noted before, it is common for many of our audience members to have studied English in schools with large classes where opportunities to speak are limited. These are the non-native English speakers who can read and write the language with proficiency but feel insecure when speaking it. Writing a question with a grammatical error or two is usually preferable to speaking these errors in front of hundreds of people. When we read the question back to the group, we can easily correct any grammatical errors we encounter in the written question.

Example:

[Question]

"My director want that I know when begin the new project."

[Paraphrase]

"The question is, 'My director wants to know when the new project will begin.' "

Other advantages to distributing cards for questions are that they give people more time to form their questions; they avoid allowing only the most fluent speakers to ask questions; and they eliminate the need for microphones in the audience. The cards should be distributed before the presentation to save time. As part of our opening remarks, we can ask the audience to wait until the end of the presentation to ask questions and inform them that cards have been provided for this purpose.

When Soliciting Questions in Writing, Ask the Audience to Print the Questions in Uppercase Letters

It is difficult to read handwriting. Also, as noted in the comments on visual aids, the script for writing lowercase letters varies from country to country, rendering it difficult or impossible to read someone's handwriting without time to study it. Before the question-and-answer session, we can print a question in uppercase letters on a visual aid to illustrate to the audience how we want them to write their questions.

Be Concise

Long-winded answers discourage questions. We have talked a lot about the problems of communicating in another language, but this does not mean that everyone in the cross-lingual audience is silently praying that we will rescue them from having to speak English. Our audience members have invested considerable time and effort to learn our language. Many of them like to speak English and are proud of their ability to do so. The question-and-answer period is their opportunity to express themselves in English, and we shouldn't dominate the time allotted.

Decide Prior to the Presentation Whether to Entertain Questions During the Presentation or Afterward

Whether to take questions from the audience during or after the presentation depends on the following factors:

Purpose:

- Is this situation formal or informal?
- Is this a working session to define issues and arrive at solutions together or a meeting to present already formulated ideas?
- Are we interested in interaction and participation or in resolution?

Time:

- Do we have a limited amount of time to present our ideas?

- Will this be our only opportunity to speak to this group on this issue?

Logistics:

- Is it a small group or a large group?
- Do we need to use a microphone?
- What kind of visual aids are we using?
- What time of day/night are we speaking?
- How many speakers have preceded and will follow us?

In the following circumstances, it is best to ask people to hold their questions until the end of the presentation:

- When it is a formal presentation
- When we are presenting already formulated ideas for input and/or action
- When we are interested in resolution rather than process
- When we have a limited amount of time (less than a half hour)
- When we will not have another opportunity to speak to the group
- When the audience is large (seventy-five people or more)
- When a microphone is required
- When our visual aids are slides or videos

In the following circumstances, we may wish to answer questions from the audience as they arise:

- When the presentation is informal

- When we are interested in having everyone's opinion
- When process is more important than resolution
- When we have a lot of time to discuss issues
- When we have an ongoing relationship with the group
- When the group is small
- When our visual aids are easy to rearrange if the question requires us to change sequence (flip charts or overheads)

The major disadvantages of accepting questions during the presentation are:

- People often ask a question about something we intend to cover at a later point in the presentation.
- Ideas get raised out of sequence, which makes it harder for the cross-lingual audience to follow, understand, and retain them.
- The context can be muddled by untimely questions, making comprehension more difficult for the cross-lingual audience.
- Questions eat time. We may have to cut out important parts of our presentation to accommodate questions.
- The speaker may lose control of the group and the presentation.
- It is not unusual to have someone in an audience who asks questions out of a neurotic need to be the center of attention or to monopolize conversation.

The primary disadvantage of waiting until the end of the presentation to allow the audience to pose questions is that a major point requiring clarification may get lost. One strategy for avoiding this problem is to entertain *only* questions of clarification during the presentation.

Example:
"I'll speak for fifteen to twenty minutes and then will answer your questions. Please stop me if I talk too fast or use a word that you don't understand and need to know."

This is a good strategy because we acknowledge up front that we may inevitably use words that a non-native English speaker cannot be expected to understand. This awareness on our part may be all that is necessary to liberate the audience to participate. It seems to be human nature, or perhaps more accurately, learned behavior, that in group situations, many people will not admit that they did not understand something. More commonly, when people do not get something, they assume they are the only ones who did not understand, and prefer to sit silently with their lack of understanding rather than run the risk of appearing stupid. With the cross-lingual audience, we can help diffuse this tendency by staying focused on the audience rather than ourselves, and using our eye contact to continually read the faces of our listeners for signs of incomprehension. Blank stares, forced grins, and knitted brows often broadcast confusion. When we are certain that we see these signs, or even if we only have a hunch, it pays to smoothly intervene with a comprehension check.

Example:
"Is there anything that you don't understand about step three in the conversion process?"

If there are no questions, it never hurts to reiterate or paraphrase an important point. If our intervention instead produces a question that is not a point of clarification and could take the presentation off track, we can politely ask the questioner to hold the question until the end of the presentation.

Example:
"That's an important question, but I'd like to wait until the end of the presentation to answer it. Are there any other questions about step three?"

8

Telephoning

Talking on the telephone is possibly the most challenging task for the non-native English speaker. The good news for us is that, as noted earlier, the secretaries who answer our phone calls are often the most fluent in English. While their business and professional colleagues have been busy studying marketing strategies, budget analyses, and organizational flow charts, many of the secretaries have been studying languages. The bad news is that we cannot always count on being connected with a secretary who speaks English as well or better than we do, and sooner or later, our call will be passed on to someone whose level of fluency does not approach the secretary's. If we regularly have phone contact with the same people, we should quickly develop a sense of how well they understand us, and hopefully, we will have established a close enough relationship to good-naturedly ride together over the potholes in our communication. There are, however, countless situations where the language barrier is infinitely greater when the communicating parties are talking by telephone.

I give a course exclusively on telephone communication, and I asked my clients to list those factors beyond the language itself that make telephone communication tedious for them. Let us first examine what these factors are, and then we will address what we can do to surmount them.

Difficulties in Telephone Communication

There Are No Visual Cues

The valuable information conveyed by gestures and facial expression are unavailable to us when we talk on the telephone. This robs the non-native English speaker of important visual cues for clarifying meaning, and it robs us of the necessary visual cues for their comprehension.

Telephone Calls Are Often Interruptive

Occasionally, telephone calls are planned. Dr. Wong is expecting us to call at 4 P.M. to discuss the linear accelerator. More often than not, however, telephone calls arrive when the non-native speaker is involved in something else, most probably, conducting business in his or her own language. The speaker must immediately shift gears and begin thinking in English. Even clients with a good fluency level have told me that when they have not been speaking English for a while, it takes them a few minutes before they feel competent in English.

There May Be Technical Difficulties

The quality of international telephone lines, even in this day and age of communication satellites, varies from country to country and region to region. International calls can be marred by weak lines, crossed lines, static, and delays on the line. These problems are frustrating when language is not a factor, but when the communication is cross-lingual, they are problematic as well as irritating.

Telephone Calls Often Take Place in a Highly Distracting Environment

Competing noises from office machines, the conversations of other colleagues in the office, and other telephone calls create a cacophony of sound that interferes with the non-native English speaker's ability to concentrate on us. In addition, people who do not have private offices have to field our telephone call while impatient colleagues are dropping things on their desk, taking things from their desk, writing notes for them, and sending them nonverbal messages about something they want. Secretaries commonly have to juggle several telephone calls simultaneously. These intrusions are not peculiar to the work environment of the non-native English speaker. They happen everywhere, but their power to distract and defeat communication assumes a much greater magnitude in a cross-lingual situation.

Lack of Privacy Can Intimidate the Non-Native English Speaker

"I do pretty well speaking English on the phone if I am alone," one of my clients said, "but if someone is standing around listening to me, even if they don't understand English, I simply block." Unfortunately, part of the baggage that comes with adulthood is a certain degree of self-consciousness. We do not want to embarrass or make fools of ourselves. This is the anxiety that causes so many of us to be afraid of speaking before groups. For the non-native English speaker, talking on the phone in English while other people are around feels like a performance. Inevitably, the situation makes non-native English speakers split their attention between the phone call and the "audience." This can be even more stressful if the non-native English speaker is a top manager and the "audience" is a subordinate. The possibility of losing face is greater.

Fortunately, most top managers have their own offices, but frequently they have to take international calls while they are in conference with staff members. When I first arrived in Europe and had to limp my way through phone calls in a foreign language, I used to ask my colleague to leave the room while I was on the phone. Many non-native English speakers, however, work in large offices that do not permit them this option.

Guidelines for Telephone Communication

Speak Slowly and Enunciate Clearly

In the absence of visual cues, the words and the voice assume greater importance. Many of us speak too rapidly on the phone, as we have no visual feedback to remind us to slow down. My clients report that when they ask native English speakers to speak more slowly, inevitably we begin the next sentence or two more slowly and then quickly begin to race again as though it were the Indianapolis 500. We should put a sign on our desk that says, "Speak slowly," and look at it periodically from the moment we dial the international access code until the end of the call.

If the Telephone Connection Is Bad, Offer to Call Back

It is not uncommon for us to assume that occasional bad intercontinental telephone connections are to be expected and that we simply have to put up with them. What is merely irritating to us, however, may be a major obstacle to the non-native English speaker. Usually, a redial is sufficient to correct the disturbance.

Identify Yourself and Your Company and Offer to Spell Both

We usually open a phone call by saying something like: "Good morning. This is Marcy Stuart of the Bonker Corporation. I'd like to speak to Mr. Brown, please." If Mr. Brown is in the office, no problem. If he is not available, however, the person taking the call may ask for the phone number and a message, and try to phonetically approximate the name and the company rather than asking for it. I have heard people commonly ask for all this information when they are taking a call in their own language yet omit it when the incoming call is in English. First, they assume that they should have understood, and second, they are often flustered by the language and are seeking the relief of the dial tone as soon as possible. To avoid this, we should offer to spell our name and company before we ask for the person with whom we want to speak.

Example:

"Good morning. I'm Marcy Stuart of the Bonker Corporation. Let me spell that. It's Marcy, M-A-R-C-Y, Stuart, S-T-U-A-R-T, of the Bonker Corporation, B-O-N-K-E-R. May I speak to Mr. Brown, please?"

This procedure ensures that if Mr. Brown is in, he will get the correct name and company of the caller. If he is not in, two essential pieces of information have already been supplied to the person taking the call, who can then devote more attention to other details when we leave our message.

We need to be aware that names that we may think are simple are not so clear-cut for a non-native English speaker. English is not a phonetic language and has many spelling eccentricities. Also, names like Stuart have more than one spelling *(Stewart)*.

We must also pay attention to the words we use to clarify an alphabetical letter or we may end up like Mike Nichols in the classic Mike Nichols/Elaine May telephone routine where he spells the name of the party whose number he wants with clarifiers like *p* as in *pneumonia* or *k* as in *knife.* We should select simple, basic words that even someone with a low English fluency level will understand—words that could be found in a children's book and refer to common objects or frequently used verbs, adjectives, and adverbs:

A as in APPLE
B as in BALL
C as in CAT
D as in DOG
E as in EAT
F as in FOOD
G as in GOOD

Spell Words with Double Letters by Saying "Double" Plus the Letter

The British would more commonly say, *"Potter*—that's P-O-DOUBLE T-E-R." The Americans more commonly say, "That's P-O-T-T-E-R." Though I generally give no preference to British English habits over the American or vice versa, in this particular instance I feel the British way of spelling will prevent the possibility that the person taking the message thinks we have simply repeated the double letter, and so he or she writes it as one. The same advice holds for double numbers, for example, 4-7-3-DOUBLE-9-5-0-6.

Concisely State the Purpose of the Call

Too often we confuse the purpose of our call with the content of our call. It is quite similar to the distinction we made between the *subject* of our speech and the *content* of the speech. Our objective is to not overload the person who answers the phone with the information that properly belongs to the person with whom we want to speak.

Example:
  "I'm calling about the press conference on Thursday."

[instead of]

Example:
  "I'm calling because I want to know how many people are going to be at the press conference on Thursday and whether he has invited the managers from the subsidiaries, and if so how many?"

The information in the second example is relevant only if we need to leave a message, in which case we should tighten it up.

Example:
"Please ask him to call me back today. I want to know: (1) How many people will be at the press conference? (2) Has he invited managers from the subsidiaries? and (3) If yes, how many?

Repeat Phone Numbers and Ask to Have Them Repeated Back

If names are misspelled in a telephone message, the consequences will not necessarily be negative unless we are asking them to send something to us. Phone numbers must be accurate. When we leave our phone number, we should give it in units, repeat it, and ask the person to read it back to us.

Example:
"The number is: country code double-zero-4-9/ the area code is 7-4-6/ and the number is: 9-8-6/4-3-2-7. That's double-zero-4-9/7-4-6/9-8-6/4-3-2-7. Could you read that back to me, please?"

English-language textbooks teach that the Americans say *zero* and the British say *0*, as in *Oh*. In my experience, we use them interchangeably. *Zero* is probably less apt to be confused by the non-native English speaker.

Note the Difference in Stress Between Numbers Ending in -teen and Numbers Ending in -ty

Non-native English speakers have trouble distinguishing between numbers like *fifteen* and *fifty*. We are often responsible for their difficulty because we are not distinct in our pronunciation.

The numbers between thirteen and nineteen have their stress on the second syllable: thir*teen*, four*teen*, fif*teen*. The voice should rise on the second syllable. The numbers ending in *-ty* place their stress on the first syllable: *thir*ty, *for*ty, *fif*ty. The voice rises on the first syllable and drops on the second. The difference in sound is quite subtle, but the repercussions can be quite large.

Pay Special Attention to "Sixes" and "Sevens"

Perhaps the reason for the saying, "I'm at sixes and sevens," as an expression for confusion has its roots in the fact that these numbers are often confused. I won't hazard a guess as to why. I only know that my non-native-English-speaking clients mix them up. If we are dealing in sixes and sevens, we can first be aware that the potential for mistakes is there and have the people we are talking to confirm what they have heard so that we can correct them if necessary. Second, when giving phone numbers and addresses, we can say *one-seven* instead of *seventeen*, or *six-zero* instead of *sixty*.

Clearly Pronounce Tuesday *and* Thursday *and Provide the Date as Well as the Day When Taking and Giving Messages*

The *th* sound is quite strange for non-native English speakers and one of the hardest to pronounce. Sticking one's tongue out to speak strikes many as a bizarre thing to do. As a result, the days of the week, *Tuesday* and *Thursday*, sound similar to a non-native English ear and are often pronounced almost identically. To avoid

waiting outside a restaurant in the rain on Tuesday
night for someone who won't arrive until Thursday, we
should ask for the date as well as the day when taking
or leaving a message, and confirm it.

Example:
  "So that's Thursday, January 10th, is that right?"

Be Aware of International Time Differences When Leaving Messages

Fortunately, if we fail to consider the time difference
when we call an office, the only thing we wake up at 4
A.M. is the answering machine. Most of us are aware of
time zones when we make the telephone call, but we
can be imprecise when we leave a message. We should
always specify when we can be called back and indicate
whether it is our time or their time.

Use the Twenty-Four-Hour International Clock or Specify A.M. and P.M.

Most countries tell time with a twenty-four-hour clock,
so that 7 P.M. is 1900 hours. Although the international
influence of the United States is tempering this practice,
it remains a good idea to use the twenty-four-hour clock
because it leaves less room for error. If we stay with the
twelve-hour clock, we should always specify A.M. or P.M.
unless the context makes it obvious. Someone who
shows up for a breakfast meeting at 8:00 at night is "out
to lunch" rather than breakfast.

Ask People to "Hold" or "Hold On" Rather Than "Hang On"

"Please hold," or "Can you hold on?" are widely taught
and understood expressions in EFL/ESL courses. "Hang

on," however, is an idiomatic phrasal verb that is too quickly mistaken for "hang up." Our non-native English speakers know that "hang up" means "put the phone down," but few know that "hang on" means "hold." A Hungarian friend spent her first several weeks in New York slamming down the phone every time someone asked her to "hang on." She thought that Americans were the rudest people she had ever encountered until she learned that they didn't mean "hang up."

9

Using an Interpreter

We are all familiar with the cliche, "It loses something in the translation." What we may not know is that the amount and the importance of what gets lost depends on us as much as on the interpreter. There are three kinds of interpretation: (1) simultaneous, (2) consecutive, and (3) chuchotage.

Simultaneous Translation

Simultaneous translation is most frequently used in high-level international communication situations, for example, encounters between heads of state. All participants wear headphones and an interpreter simultaneously translates the words of the sender into the language of the receiver. For example, when Chancellor Kohl speaks, an interpreter translates his words from German into English for President Clinton while another interpreter is translating the same words into French for President Mitterand. If a speech has been prepared and written word-for-word, the interpreter may have access to the text beforehand. Generally, however, the interpreter does not have a text and must translate as the speaker speaks. This is no light task for the interpreter. Structural differences in languages pose significant challenges.

The first challenge is word order. In English, for example, our adjectives usually precede the nouns they modify. In many other languages, they come after the word they modify. In German, the verb often comes at the end of the sentence. Syntactical differences such as these require the interpreter to hear an entire sentence before it can be accurately translated. The interpreter has to sustain this delay in hearing the sender's message and then pronounce the sentence in the language of the receiver without losing the subsequent sentence of the sender. This dynamic demands that we speak more slowly and use the pause as spoken punctuation to allow our interpreter to translate us faithfully. Simultaneous interpreters cite John F. Kennedy as an excellent example of a speaker who was easy to interpret, owing to his frequent use of the pause.

Consecutive Translation

Consecutive translation is used in one-on-one encounters and frequently in meetings and on television. In consecutive translation, there are no headphones and no interpreters sequestered in booths. The interpreter is present, using shorthand to capture the words of the speaker, which the interpreter translates at intervals.

Several years ago, the Lord Mayor of London was visiting Rome. It was mostly a ceremonial visit. The major Italian state television station invited her as a guest on the afternoon news broadcast. I expect they invited her out of respect for her position and possibly because

she was a great dresser. They certainly were not re-
questing her thinking on lofty political issues because
the question they asked her was, "How does London
deal with heavy traffic?" It is fortunate that she was not
asked to comment on a more controversial issue because
the Italians never got to hear her answer—not in Italian,
that is. She talked nonstop for nearly two minutes,
oblivious to the efforts of the interpreter to interrupt
and translate what she had said to the television audience. To help the consecutive translator, we need to develop the skill of speaking concisely and stopping periodically to give the translator the opportunity to
translate us.

I see a lot of English speakers translated in Italy. By
far the most accomplished user of consecutive translation I have ever seen is the American writer Gore Vidal.
He delivers several sentences, then stops, awaits the
translation, and begins again. Watching him with the
consecutive translator is like watching a beautifully cho-
reographed dance. We need to remind ourselves, however, that in a consecutive translation situation, we are
Fred Astaire and the translator is Ginger Rogers.

Chuchotage

Chuchotage is the French word for "whisper." We
might encounter an interpreter using this technique if
we are the only person or perhaps one of two people
who do not speak the native language of the assembled
group. We will be seated next the interpreter. The interpreter conveys the gist of the group conversation going
on around us so that we can understand the proceedings. When we want to contribute to the discussion, the

interpreter then switches to consecutive interpretation to translate us to the others.

The Press Conference

An international press conference can be a bit like a three-ring circus. When President Clinton and President Yeltsin communicate the outcome of a summit meeting, customarily they wear headphones and simultaneous interpreters translate Clinton's comments to Yeltsin and vice versa. Sometimes the press corps also has headphones and is privy to the simultaneous translation, but often the press is (1) expected to be fluent in the language of the interlocutors or (2) there is a supplementary consecutive translation in English, the international language. Generally, top-level international meetings with heads of state are well coordinated in terms of interpreting services because the power and resources to provide them exist, the experience is vast, and the negative repercussions of misunderstandings are great. International press conferences at a less lofty level, however, do not always take into account the vast range of linguistic needs.

Several years ago, a multinational record company held a press conference to announce the much-awaited release of a CD (compact disc) series of a revered classical master. A significant amount of time and money was dedicated to putting the press conference together. The conference was organized by the U.S. headquarters of the company even though the press conference took place in a European capital. The entire press conference was conducted in English. This posed no problem for the international journalists who spoke English, but the organizers did not take into account that the audience would be full of local journalists, most of whom did not speak English. The triumph of the CD release was overshadowed by the disgruntled feelings of the local journalists who had had to sit through a press conference without understanding most of what was said. As a result, the stories about the CD release in the national newspapers focused almost exclusively on this faux pas and dedicated little or no attention to the CD release. The strongest criticisms charged "American arrogance" and "linguistic imperialism."

There is one foolproof way to ensure that this never happens: *Start where the audience is.* This brings us full-circle to where this book began, and rightly so. The distinction between master carpenters and those of us who just pound boards together is that master carpenters know their wood. They know what tool to use on which surface. In the final analysis, all the techniques at our disposal will be of no avail if we do not *know* our audience. *Start where the audience is!* It is the alpha and the omega of communicating successfully in a cross-lingual environment.

Index

abbreviations, avoiding,
44–45
abstract terms, defining,
43–44
acronyms, avoiding, 44–45
action step(s), 23–29
benefits to audience of taking, 26–29
characteristics of, 24–25
defined, 24
examples of, 25–29, 37
statement of, 34
active vocabulary, 87
American English, British
English vs., 65–66
analogies, 30
indigenous to audience,
48–49
anecdotes, 30, 33
Aristotle, on nonverbal communication, 52–53
articulation
of consonants, 68–69
elisions in, 69
of vowels, 67–68

attention-getting opening, 32
audience analysis, 18–22
action step(s) and, 25–29
attitudes toward speaker,
19, 20
during demonstrations,
92–93
to develop examples and
analogies, 48–49
English-language profi-
ciency, 20–22
for feedback, 59–60,
74–75, 94
knowledge of subject, 20
mingling in, 22
motivation of audience,
20, 26–29
nature of audience, 19
audience participation,
105–111
demonstrations in, 92–93,
106
encouraging, 110–111
facilitating, 107–111
in group discussions, 111